Queerying
Occultures

Some Other Titles from Falcon Press

Phil Hine
> *Condensed Chaos: An Introduction to Chaos Magic*
> *Prime Chaos: Adventures in Chaos Magic*
> *The Pseudonomicon*
> *Hine's Varieties: Chaos & Beyond*

Gregory Peters
> *Yogini Magic: The Sorcery, Enchantment & Witchcraft of the Divine Feminine*

Christopher S. Hyatt, Ph.D.
> *Undoing Yourself with Energized Meditation & Other Devices*
> *Secrets of Western Tantra: The Sexuality of the Middle Path*
> *The Big Black Book*

Christopher S. Hyatt, Ph.D. with contributions by Wm. S. Burroughs, Timothy Leary, Robert Anton Wilson et al.
> *Rebels & Devils: The Psychology of Liberation*

S. Jason Black and Christopher S. Hyatt, Ph.D.
> *Tantra without Tears*
> *Pacts with the Devil: A Chronicle of Sex, Blasphemy & Liberation*
> *Urban Voodoo: A Beginner's Guide to Afro-Caribbean Magic*

Antero Alli
> *Angel Tech: A Modern Shaman's Guide to Reality Selection*
> *Experiential Astrology: From the Map to the Territory*

Peter J. Carroll
> *The Chaos Magick Audios*
> *PsyberMagick*

Joseph Lisiewski, Ph.D.
> *Ceremonial Magic and the Power of Evocation*
> *Kabbalistic Cycles and the Mastery of Life*
> *Kabbalistic Handbook for the Practicing Magician*

Israel Regardie
> *The Complete Golden Dawn System of Magic*
> *The Golden Dawn Audios*
> *The World of Enochian Magic (audio)*

Denny Sargent
> *Naga Magick: The Wisdom of the Serpent Lords*

Steven Heller
> *Monsters & Magical Sticks: There's No Such Thing As Hypnosis?*

For up-to-the-minute information on prices and availability, please visit our website at
http://originalfalcon.com

Queerying Occultures

Essays from Enfolding Vol. 1

Phil Hine

Foreword by
Patricia MacCormack

THE *Original* FALCON PRESS
TEMPE, ARIZONA, U.S.A.

International Standard Book Number: 978-1-61869-793-6
ISBN: 978-1-61869-795-0 (mobi)
ISBN: 978-1-61869-796-7 (ePub)
Library of Congress Catalog Card Number: 2022952432

First Edition 2023
First eBook Edition 2023

Cover artwork "Snails in Love" by Maria Strutz.
https://maria-strutz.onlineweb.shop/

The paper used in this publication meets the minimum requirements of the American National Standard for Permanence of Paper for Printed Library Materials Z39.48-1984

Address all inquiries to:
The Original Falcon Press
1753 East Broadway Road #101-277
Tempe, AZ 85282 U.S.A.
(or)
PO Box 3540
Silver Springs NV 89429 U.S.A.

website: **http://www.originalfalcon.com**
email: info@originalfalcon.com

Acknowledgements

With thanks to Patricia MacCormack for her erudite *Foreword* and continued support. To Mat Auryn, Amy Hale and especially Lou Hart for her memoir of Queer Pagan Camp. To David Southwell for much-valued criticism. To Maria Strutz for her cover painting, and for putting up with me for the last thirty years or so.

Thanks also to all those who listened to my ravings, have encouraged me to write and supported me through times both good and bad. In particular: Jenny Alexander, Gavin Brown, Chris Hubley, Joseph De Lappe, Paul McAndrew, Brooke Palmieri, Estelle Seymour, Gordon the Toad, and Nick Tharcher. Last but not least, the Treadwell's Bookshop crew, past and present.

— *Phil Hine, London, 2022*

Contents

One:
Queerying Paganisms

Two:
Queerying Tantras

Three:
Queerying Histories

Foreword

In many ways, the title of Phil Hine's *Queerying Occultures* describes the uncapturable nature of this lifelong project, or a project of a way of living. Occulture suggests a monolithic homogenous system, a closed circuit which demarcates a single way of being in the world as a practitioner of magick, and who experiences the world as magical. Yet one of Hine's most enigmatic contributions to magick exceeds a sense of occulture. It is inclusive of all life and ways of living as being somehow both inherently magick and banal, each encounter or practice a moment of potential for thinking, doing and living with chaos as a liberating force. The grandiosity, the awe-invoking elements of chaos rituals and ancient entities live alongside domestic existence and humble actions, and without hierarchy both are encountered with equal wonderment, a chaotic remapping of what could be an atrophied scenario.

Nothing escapes enchantment for Hine, neither practitioner, encounter nor idea. Further than the richness of a life offering the grand alongside the immediate and mild, Hine attests, without hierarchy or prioritisation, to the being-within-all of the great and the modest, the grim and the delightful, the perverse and the boring. Hine shows the necessity of escaping the will to categorization, taxonomy, right and wrong, beloved of the Anthropos, and (usually) his being in magick. The melding of Lovecraftian ancients with the overwhelming simplicity of, for example, a kiss, enhances awareness of the powers and vulnerabilities and reorientations of self that occur in so many ways under every context. Taking thought and life away from structure and status also takes magick from order, showing chaos as a force of liberation under every context. For chaos, the powers which constitute Anthropos are not simply defunct, they're as tedious as they are unappealing—power as domination, reproduction of the same (be it ritual or affect), payoffs and outcomes utterly predictable. Because Anthropos sets himself as conjurer of a world external, while chaos delights in our immersion within, through and as the world, each ritualistic projection a way to navigate, disorganise and reorganise our own expression and perception of the world to elicit wondrous new modes of thinking, divested of the power implicit in utilising knowledge for gain.

To return to the title, the world of chaos is simultaneously us (the multiples that make us, the us within a multiply occupied group, coven or ritual) and we emerge through new manifestations in and of the world, in trembling, the 'knowledge trembling in secret' of which Hine speaks—and we are never extricated from that existence as trembling, the secret which cannot be exposed, that is a material, visceral incarnation of the never-to-be-revealed but that is encountered nonetheless. This ecosophy of connections between ideas, bodies and worldings is existence as active enfoldings, a world of flows rather than of dialectics.

Critically Hine works with the role of desire in occulture. Desire for the chaotic indulges our enfoldings in order to pique all modes of desire as force and affect, beyond dualisms of power and submission, manipulation and subtlety, even the pleasurable and the despairful. Just as desire has no single quality but is always multiple and in excess of its own ability to be known—the knowledge trembling in secret— so too are we, and so Hine reminds us it is not the magician who wields power to create the world, but desire itself that makes the magician and the world manifest, beyond our capacity to fully exhaust its meaning. In this sense, if Anthropos is the male, heteronormative magus who creates causal results in the world (and their connection with a form of transcendental neo-capitalism) then chaos queers us as it que(e)ries the purpose of occultism. Like revealing one's own desires from the closet by announcing a reified sexuality that ossifies desire into an acceptable model, there is not much left of the 'secret' of occultism in Anthropos-oriented magick, beyond possibly its selfish hoarding of secrets as objects. Queer magick queries the coming out at all, because the potential for transparent revelation simply is not there—chaos makes all revelations temporary and tactical. We as magi query ourselves, our relationships with the effects of the world, occulture itself, always present in the formal-informality of Hine's DIY meets sacred incitements to create rituals how and where and in whatever manner we can, querying magick's own occasional leanings to regimental or even ecumenical strictness.

The becomings of ourselves via our queer desires finds historical and global encounters in this book with the fascinating examples of the manifold genders, sexualities and practices of shamanism, tantra, paganism, god and corpse deities that don't simply breakdown the sorting of licit from illicit, but life from death and perception from reality. With sensitivity and devoid of co-option, Hine explores shared intensities of becomings from different eras and esoteric practices, utilising varied fabulations such as Baphomet and Ardhanarishvara, that remind us the single-gendered, heteronormative model of human subjectivity is highly contemporary as a concept, and ultimately no more or less a mythical fabulation than any other godmonsters. In this ethical turn, Hine is able to unravel and reravel the urgency with which we need to queer ourselves, our relationship with power and pleasure, examining not only our will to categorise and manipulate, but what is lost and left out by designating such concepts as gender and desire as themselves able to be categorised at all. For just as some subjects are left out, left over, denied, so too concepts which are denied their chaos are drained of vitality. We are the left out and the left overs, and thrive in being such.

The joyful ethics of the feminist, queer ethos of *Queerying* reminds the occultist that just as the sexuality of women was decried as witchcraft, and the sexuality of queer folk repudiated as turpitude, what Anthropos fears is what chaos experimenters covet: the trembling fear that is always at the heart of even the most jubilant ritual, the moment of opening during the homoerotic kiss, the loss of self in the flourishing becoming-multiple of denouncing gender norms and presentations, the vulnerability that is its own kind of power in embracing the grotesque, being the grotesque and not apologising, or mimicking the dominant to access their kind of power.

The personal vulnerabilities, being the everyday lives, of occultists is also not left out in Hine's work. The chaos in which Spare lived with easels, paint and cats everywhere is accompanied in *Queerying* with tantalising examples of possible real-life crossings between Austin Osman Spare and the Bloomsbury set, where occultism is found in chance encounters (which may or may not be apocryphal), and polyvocality from art, literature, politics and philosophy, amalgamating as the single expression of life found in the coagulation of the many within cities, as well as the unlike-becomings between types—identities, individuals, even species or pantheons—that shouldn't go together. Just as chaos is everywhere, so too queer is not confined to the private space, but to all unlike-encounters that swell our capacity to be affected while reminding us of our vulnerability, a critical aspect of all curiosity. Hine teases this vulnerability in the writings here, through graphic descriptions of experiences benign and tempestuous, showing queer in a kaleidoscopic series of overlapping fractals designed not to exemplify nor even less to normalise, only to show that the world and our thoughts are already too much for normative human subjectivity manifest as Anthropos.

Is the purpose of magick to tame through knowledge, transcend this world, or does that reek of the superstition of unenlightened magi who were acolytes of Descartes and Rousseau as much as a Judeo-Christian god? The great heretics were experimenters with the very possibility of thinking, the world already too much and they wanting to immerse themselves in the too much (or as William Blake says: 'Too much! But not enough!'). Reducing the world by converting it to human knowledge enhances Anthropos, the man astride the world. This dismisses the spectre of nature that is increasingly important today, and it leaves the whole cosmos out, which of course would deny us chaos practitioners most of our Elder gods and Ancient Ones (I write with a smirk). Chaos gods are concepts, fabulations as problems, which is the reason for and meaning of concepts according to Deleuze and Guattari. Just as women, queers, hybrids and other chaos collectives have created problems for Anthropos, so chaos magick creates problems that we may explore the Earth, the cosmos, differently. Rituals and fabulations have affects that are less relevant as true or false than they are as altering pathways of knowledge by exploding them into multiple lines of flight of thinking-otherwise.

And following from Irigaray, in chaos magick these lines of flight are sticky, mucosal ones leading directly to the gods. Chaos' fabulated gods exist only, for Hine, as "the seething exuberance of life exceeding all limitations, refusing to be chained by expectations and definitions, escaping limitations and overflowing any attempt to categorise and capture." Gods resisting iconography, chaos practitioners resisting atrophied subjectivity, though Hine here speaks of Baphomet, this entire work takes us and the gods and our indeterminable connectivity with both as this seething exuberance. It is, indeed, the Twilight of the Gods, but only those gods anthropocentrics have formed themselves as, while destroying the world. We queer chaos experimenters exist with our gods, though none of us exist in the strictest sense, or more than the most infinitesimal moment. As we are visceral, seething, teeming, mucosal flesh, we are also shimmering, kissing, dreamed, fleeting concepts. In these pages, Hine puts his flesh where his ideas are, speaking intimately and in abstract concepts without dividing the two. The pages before you are as much a call to ethical experiments in magick and in experiencing the world as they are examples of miracles of strangeness which are here, now, for us to indulge in, slaying the arrogant Anthropos through queerying one kind of perception of the world, and opening ourselves and our connectivities to infinite other perceptions.

— *Patricia MacCormack*

Introduction

Welcome to *Queerying Occultures,* the first volume of an occasional series: *Essays from Enfolding. Enfolding.org,* the blog where I have held forth on a semi-regular basis since 2009, was initially conceived as a group project. Unfortunately, shortly after its launch, many of the original contributors had to back away to work on more pressing projects, and I was left to fill the void with occasional guest posts from friends. I wanted to use *enfolding* to explore a variety of topics and themes that had been increasingly occupying me since the beginning of the noughties, such as my interest in obscure corners of history—the relationship between esotericism and colonialism, and an in-depth engagement with the literature, philosophy and practice of the tantric traditions which I had been following since the late 1980s. Disparate as these themes are, I started to see connections, although it is often akin to doing a jigsaw puzzle without the benefit of knowing what the final picture should look like. The joy is in the momentary sliding together of pieces—the hints and glimpses of something larger forming out of disconnected fragments.

The essays that make up *Queerying Occultures* were—with a few exceptions—written between 2010 and 2020. They are arranged into three thematic sections (although there is some overlap among them). Rather than bedazzle the reader with one huge Bibliography at the end of the book, I have closed each section with its own Bibliography.

The *Prologue* essay, *Queer and Loathing in Twentieth-Century Occultism* is a personal reflection of the occult homophobia of the

1980s–90s, which was alas, an all too common experience on the UK's occult scene. I attempt to explore the roots of this homophobia in occult discourse, and trace how far we've got beyond it.

The first section, *Queerying Paganisms,* is a disparate collection of musings, reflections and interrogations on various aspects of 'Queer Paganism.' The second group of essays, *Queerying Tantras,* emerged out of my engagement with Tantra as a practice, and what it might mean to 'queer' those practices and perspectives. The third section, *Queerying Histories,* highlights various historical moments that I feel are useful in thinking about the development of queer esoteric narratives.

§§§

To name myself queer is, for me, less about a certain mode of being, and more an ethical position with which to engage the world.

I sometimes wonder if queer is 'untranslatable,' given its refusal to be trapped by binary thinking. The dualistic categorization of objects and subjects into dichotomous opposites has, all too often, proved to be the lynchpin underwriting systems of race, class and gender oppression. As activist bell hooks put it, such thinking is "the central ideological component of all systems of domination in Western society."[1]

Consider dichotomies such as white/black, male/female, reason/emotion, fact/feeling, spirit/matter, higher/lower, magic/mundane, straight/gay. All gain their meaning in relation to the difference of their oppositional counterparts. All too frequently the opposites do not support each other, but rather they are inherently opposed—one

---

[1] hooks, 1984, p29. "bell hooks" (deliberately written in lower case), is the pen name of the late Gloria Jean Watkins (1952–2021).

superior, the other inferior. One half is dominant, the other half, subjugated. White is superior to black; facts are superior to feelings; spirit is elevated over mere materiality. Breaking out of such traps and their 'occult' equivalents was an early lesson for me and other queer friends. Over time, I have come to understand the benefits of an intersectional approach, both as an analytic tool and a mode of ethical engagement. One of the characteristics of intersectionality is an attention to difference and complexity, as important as the focus on social inequality and structures of oppression. There is a demand that we pay attention to everyday, lived experience; that people's lives and their accounts of those lives matter; to understand identities without falling back into preconceived and master narratives of values, politics and ideologies. To understand that queer—and intersectionality as a project in its myriad, chimeric forms—may well be a work in progress rather than a reified given.

§§§

What does it entail, to Queery Occultures? I confess, at this juncture, I don't exactly know. But I suspect it involves more than an easy assimilation into mainstream Paganism and Occultism, or the breaking away to create new enclaves and safe spaces. I have little personal interest in 'queering' existing occult narratives, fruitful though that may be, but I recognize the value of doing so. Rather, it is my hope that new avenues—new lines of flight—will open up, if we can at least take time to dream of them.

Prologue:
Queer and Loathing in
Twentieth-Century Occultism

As 2022 speeds to a close, human rights are under attack in myriad ways that seem determined to drag us back to the 1950s, if not further. The USA Supreme Court's overturning of Roe vs. Wade, guaranteeing federal constitutional protections of abortion rights in May; the escalating transphobia in European and the USA's 'culture wars'; the homophobic 'Groomer' narrative being pushed by American and British conservatives. Even the 'Satanic Panic' of the 1980s and 90s is gaining traction once more (although really, it never went away).

Histories—particularly uncomfortable histories—tend to get swept under the carpet. Ignored, all too conveniently forgotten, unspoken. For many years, the queer entanglements of occultism in the global North (particularly in the UK) were sidelined and seemingly of little interest to both scholars and practitioners alike. I can remember talking to a gay (but closeted) occultist in mid-1980s—a well-known author of several books on magic, who told me frankly that I wouldn't get any interest in a book on queer magic. "Occultists don't want to hear about queers, and queers don't want to hear about the occult," was more or less how he put it to me. He went on to tell me that in the 1960s, he'd been a member of an entirely gay ceremonial magic lodge—but that due to his 'oath of initiation' he could not say more. He also told me that if he revealed himself to be a gay magician, then no one would come to his workshops and lectures. This was not an untypical attitude in the British occult scene during the 1980s—doubtless not helped by the responses to the AIDS virus, dubbed "the gay plague" in the media. There were calls to make homosexuality illegal once more, and that AIDS victims should be interned in what was effectively, concentration camps. This was not a good time to be out as 'bi'. Bisexuals were frequently demonized as being 'worse' than Gays, as they threatened 'normal people.' The UK was also under the sway of a Conservative government keen to crack down on 'permissiveness' who, in 1988 passed the infamous Section 28—a series of laws that prohibited local authorities to publish or promote any material that promoted the concept of "homosexuality as a pretended family relationship."

On the UK's Pagan and Occult scene, didactic statements and 'occult laws' demonising anyone not heterosexual, abounded. The selection of quotations which accompany this essay were compiled by myself and Paul McAndrew in 1991. We simply went through the books on our shelves and picked out choice quotes. They show how widespread the condemnation of the non-heterosexual was in that period—Wicca, Thelema, Sacred Sex, Tantra, Ceremonial Magic, Macrobiotics; choose any tradition or spiritually-inclined genre from that time and you'd be bound to find someone making the argument that non-straight folk were beyond the pale. There was much talk of blocked chakras, reverse kundalini, plugs and sockets, and polarity—all favourite justifications for condemnation. Perhaps my 'favourite' is the one that says "homosexuals are not human"—a kind of queered-up *Invasion of the Body Snatchers*. Some magical orders openly declared they did not accept anyone who was homosexual. The High Priestess of a Wiccan coven I was in told me that anyone who was gay or bisexual could not possibly advance spiritually. People knew of Aleister Crowley's bisexuality, of the passionate homoeroticism of his *Hymn to Pan*, but that, for some at least, made Crowley all the more suspect. I remember going to a lecture about Crowley's infamous 'Choronzon Working' with Victor Neuburg in 1909. At one point the lecturer mumbled, "And we presume something homosexual took place," whereupon Paul & I, who were sitting in the front row, shouted "What? Tell us?" and the lecturer blushed and hid behind his notes.

This 'occult homophobia' gradually changed over the next two decades or so. More queer folk began to move around on the UK's occult & pagan scenes. They challenged the prevailing unthinking prejudices, often just by being present and refusing to be cowed by blatherings about polarity or blocked chakras. But it was slow going, and for some, a struggle. A trans friend was suddenly barred from going to a goddess circle (I found out, years later, that the person behind the banning was someone I had, up to that point, considered a friend). I heard of a young man who'd come out as gay to the ceremonial magic lodge which had been, up until that moment, the centre of his life. They'd ceremonially 'banished' him, and he later committed suicide. There was a woman friend who stopped going to pagan meetings and conferences because of the constant nudging and whispering about her being a lesbian. I recall visiting a local Wiccan coven in the mid-1990s, where even sharing a semi-formal chalice of wine (passed along with a chaste kiss) involved getting everyone present into a male-female chain. The one gay man in that coven told me proudly that he was 'straight' when he stepped into the circle.

> *"What people have to remember is that Wicca—man and woman, God and Goddess—is a fertility cult, a heterosexual fertility cult."*
> — Wiccan High Priest interviewed at
> *Autumn Link-Up*, 1989

> *"Thus, the blasphemy of the homosexual formula, for it denies Babalon and breeds devils in chaos."*
> — Kenneth Grant, *Nightside of Eden* (1977)

> *"...you can't work magic with a homosexual. Homosexuals just can't create a current."*
> — interviewee quoted from Tanya Luhrmann,
> *Persuasions of the Witches' Craft* (1989)

One reason that attitudes changed was the popularity of networking and grass-roots organising. By the mid-1980s, Pagans inspired by Marilyn Ferguson's 1987 book, *The Aquarian Conspiracy*, and the politically-engaged Witchcraft of Starhawk, were becoming increasingly active. These moves coincided with Pagans and Occultists becoming much more visible to the general public, amid a growing interest in ecological activism, animal rights, and alternative lifestyles. At the same time, many within the Pagan and Occult scene cherished their identification as 'outsiders,' and had little interest in engaging with the wider public.

The rise of interest in Women's Spirituality and activism also helped fuel these changes. In 1989, Gordon "the Toad" McLellan founded HOBLink, a network offering support to LGBT Pagans and Occultists, and for raising awareness of LGBT issues in the wider Pagan/Occult communities. There were HOBLink newsletters and occasional social meetings and workshops. On one occasion, HOBLink was refused the use of room space by the London Gay and Lesbian Centre because HOBLink included 'bisexuals.' In an interview in 1991, Gordon commented on the state of the Pagan scene in regard to LGBT Pagans:

> *"Some elements of the pagan community are trying to sell it as nice and safe and essentially middle-class and not at all threatening to society. They might well try to stuff us back into our broom cupboards. I think for paganism to try and present itself like that is a betrayal of what we stand for. For me, being pagan means working with the Earth, and if I try and sell myself as a nice, sweet, slightly eccentric person who's not a trouble-maker at all, then I'm betraying the Earth, because this society is destroying the Earth."*

> *"Homosexual freedom can be associated with the decline of Greece. From the first Century onward, homosexuality flourished in Rome; male prostitution developed to an extraordinary extent and another great empire fell."*
> — Nik Douglas & Penny Slinger, *Sexual Secrets* (1979)

> *"The homosexual male does not imitate the female adult when he 'camps' but the female child his mother played to him. Maturer aspects of adult love are often missing, and the homosexual couple finds difficulty in making an alliance of the sort that deepens with time."*
> — Jean Liedloff, *The Continuum Concept* (1975)

> *"Women are by nature Yin (passive, soft, centrifugal). When they become too Yang by eating too much Yang food, they become miserable ... they devote themselves to animal pets, or they turn homosexual. Their life is miserable because it violates all natural laws. The homosexual and the asexual person are the most pitiful of all—and the literature of the West is littered with their monstrosities. Sexual abnormality can be cured in time by strict adherence to the macrobiotic regime."*
> — Sakurazawa Nyoiti, *Macrobiotics* (1972)

British attitudes were also influenced to some degree by developments in North America, such as the rise of queer anthropologies, and a growing interest in the relationship between gender-variance, religion and occultism. A great deal of what was written then can now be criticised, certainly as a universalising tendency to assume that what was queer in 20th-century London, for example, could be retroactively applied to other cultures and the distant past. The notion that all myths or stories reflected modern concerns and sensibilities. But at least they showed that there were hidden histories and stories to uncover.

How did the British parochial attitude towards the place of non-straight people within occult discourse emerge? Where did it come from? We don't have to look far. The UK's occult scene in the 1980s was very different to what it is now. There was a good deal of suspicion among practitioners of different traditions and approaches. Beyond the metropolitan centres (Leeds, London, Oxford), Thelemites and Wiccans (for example) did not tend to mix much. Even owning Crowley's *Thoth* tarot deck could raise eyebrows and critical comment.

The kind of heterogenous blending of ideas that we see in modern books on Witchcraft, where an author might happily blend elements of Wicca, Chaos Magic, and Thelema into a single narrative, would have been anathema. By the same token, those who felt themselves to be 'proper' Pagans were wary of others pursuing alternative lifeways. I recall from the time I spent co-editing the zine *Pagan News,* being asked not to publish the site details of an outdoor Pagan gathering because the organisers didn't want 'New Age Travellers' turning up.

"Homosexuals cannot be true witches...we want no kinks in our circle."

— quoted from a Wiccan zine

"...homosexuality, like drugs, is a technique of black magic ... In spite of the modern state of apologetics for this form of lower emotional and physical relationship it is a perversion and evil."

— Gareth Knight, A Practical Guide to Qabalistic Symbolism (1965, 2001)

"Homosexuals are not Human. Just as Everything that glistens is not gold, similarly everyone who looks human is NOT homo sapiens. Genuine mature Human beings cannot be anything but heterosexual, for such is their nature. ... This is not a 'moral' judgement, but the fact is that there is an increasing number of non-humans 'Souls' occupying human (or should I say 'humanoid') bodies. Admittedly, most of them are just as Tellurian as men are, though from another kingdom of terrestrial human realm, as can be clearly seen from their auras. But I do not advise anyone to look at one, for it can damage the 'third eye' ..."

— Nicholas Tereshchenko, Letter, *The Lamp of Thoth* magazine

Similarly, the attention to history that is so widespread nowadays
(thanks to the work of scholars such as Owen Davies, Ronald Hutton
and Alex Owen) was not much in evidence. It now seems to me
that many of the people I knew back then operated from a predomi-
nantly 'mythic' perspective. They had little interest in history beyond
the narrative of the burning times, and when they did try to engage
with the turbulent events of that decade, they turned to the Arthurian
Myths, centering 'Great Britain' as the still vibrant heart of a spiritual
world.

The majority discourse on magic was very much couched in terms
of binary oppositions. White magic was being 'spiritual.' Focusing on
spiritual development while being largely unconcerned with everyday
life beyond immediate necessities. Black Magic, on the other hand,
was taking drugs, being involved in political activism, questioning
occult laws, not having a properly established relationship with 'inner
plane adepts'—and, of course, any kind of sexual activity beyond the
bounds of heteronormativity. When Chaos Magic began to gain
popularity in the late 1980s, the backlash from more 'traditional'
mages was palpable. William Gray, for example, in his 1989 book
Between Good and Evil: Polarities of Power (Llewellyn Publications)
drew a direct comparison between Chaos Magic and AIDS as a spiritual disease, calling Chaos Magic "anarchy" and dismissing it as
"Nuclear Nastiness."

Dion Fortune and the Left-Hand Path

The idea that involvement in politics, taking drugs, and not being
heterosexual are all indicators of 'Black Magic' (often termed 'the
Left-Hand Path') has its roots in the writings of Dion Fortune
(1890–1946). A prodigious author in her own lifetime, Fortune's
occult fiction and non-fiction have had a tremendous influence on

occultism, both in the UK and beyond. After her death in 1946, her flame was kept alive by the Society of Inner Light, and by the late Gareth Knight (1930–2022), the pen name of Basil Wilby, who published several collections of Fortune's essays and books exploring her occult beliefs and practices. Gareth Knight's bald assertion, quoted earlier, draws directly on Fortune's attitudes with his statement that homosexuality is "black magic, perversion and evil."[1]

All of the above indicators of 'black magic' can be found in Fortune's 1930 book, *Psychic Self-Defence*, still widely regarded as a classic work on self-protection against magical and human adversaries. In Chapter Five, for example, she describes the case of 'D', a youth in his late teens, "one of those degenerate but intellectual and socially presentable types" who has been suffering psychic attacks after visiting a cousin who had been invalided from the front lines during the Great War. The cousin, according to Fortune, had been caught "practising necrophilia" (not an uncommon practice, she says), and furthermore, that "the relations between D and his cousin were of a vicious nature, and one on occasion, he bit the boy on the neck, just under the ear, actually drawing blood." Relations of a

---

[1] When *A Practical Guide to Qabalistic Symbolism* was republished in 2001, Gareth Knight, in his preface, addressed his views on homosexuality.

> *"The draconian remarks on homosexuality seemed fairly commonplace at a time when this form of sexual expression was still a criminal offence. Society has since moved on quite radically in this respect; it is a cause of great regret to me if, as a result of my words, anyone has been given a bad time on account of their sexual orientation. Not that I necessarily endorse all that I see or hear about the wilder frontiers of human sexual activity, particularly when allied to quasi-magical practice (which was one of Dion Fortune's concerns) but I have no desire to set myself up as an arbiter of public morals."*

However, his original statements regarding homosexuality as 'black magic' and 'evil' remain unaltered within the body of the book.

'vicious nature' is a euphemism often associated with depravity and sexual perversity. Chapter Ten, entitled "Non-occult dangers of the Black Lodge" goes further. The 'Black Lodge' is Fortune's term for those occult fraternities engaged in either ordinary or occult criminality (sometimes both). The examples of such lodge activities include: drug trafficking, being "riddled with unnatural vice," being "little more than a house of ill-fame," and being involved with "subversive politics." On the subject of 'unnatural vice' Fortune states that there is "as much danger of corruption in a Black Lodge for boys and youths as there is for women." The police have intervened in such cases, "both here and abroad." This is a dig in the direction of the Theosophical Society, and in particular, Charles Webster Leadbeater. Fortune had joined the Christian Mystic Lodge of the Theosophical Society and became its president, but she left in the wake of the successive Leadbeater scandals.[2]

Fortune may also have been referring to a 1903 homosexual scandal—the so-called Paris *Messes Noires* ('Black Masses')—organized by the wealthy nobleman and socialite Jacques d'Adelswärd Fersen. These affairs were attended by wealthy friends of Fersen, including some Catholic priests, the main attraction being *tableau vivants* made of up of naked youths from some of the best schools in Paris. Fersen was charged with "inciting minors to debauchery," and the case was widely publicized. Fersen, who had been imprisoned for five months prior to the trial, was released afterwards, and fined 50 francs. After the trial, Fersen moved to the island of Capri, and in 1905 published *Lord Lyllian: Black Masses*—a satirical, decadent novel touching on the 1903 scandal and the trial of Oscar Wilde.

---

[2] See the essays on enfolding.org tagged 'Leadbeater' for a full exploration of this unpleasant affair. [http://enfolding.org/tag/leadbeater/]   —

In her (1929) book *Sane Occultism*, Fortune alludes to a conspiracy of male occultists who used "homosexual techniques" to build up what she called "dark astral power." In *The Esoteric Philosophy of Love and Marriage* (1922), Fortune makes her views on sexual perversions quite clear. They are the "solitary stimulation of the generative organs," and "mutual stimulation by two people of the same sex."

Fortune's *The Problem of Purity*, contains some of her theories on sexual magic as an energetic system, and discusses a practical technique for directing the sex-force to good works of selfless service, rather than dwelling on "the awful consequences its illicit uses may bring in their train."

The Doctrine of Polarity

Another lasting feature of Fortune's work is her doctrine of Polarity, which for Fortune was the key to all magical work. Fortune believed that polarity acted at all levels of existence, from the cosmological to the interpersonal, where in one instance it manifests as sex (although that is not necessarily its most important aspect). Critically—although she accepted the dominant view of the period that as far as the everyday world was concerned, men were naturally active, and women passive—she states that on the inner planes, this polarity was reversed, and that men needed women to supplement and stimulate them, both emotionally and spiritually. This theme is at the centre of Fortune's occult novels such as *The Sea Priestess* and *Moon Magic*.

It would be unfair to lay all of the twentieth-century's occult homophobia at Fortune's door, but I think it is fairly obvious that her ideas (together with other circulating notions such as 'reverse kundalini,' blocked chakras, etc., and the near-rigid enforcement of male-female pairings in Wicca) became part of the overall discourse which frowned upon the presence of non-heterosexuals in occult circles, and justified that frowning with occult theories with the status of absolute truths.

Polarity is not merely a theory; it is enacted simultaneously across multiple domains. It can, for example, be expressed spatially—where, for example, during a public ritual, men are asked to gather in one spot and women in another. Gender may be ascribed to particular ritual objects: a knife is 'male,' a cup is 'female,' for example. In Wicca, the act of consecrating wine is often understood as a symbolic act of procreation. In some traditions, there is a strong emphasis on the 'balance' between male and female polarities, that can be expressed as the ratio of male/female members within a group, or the balance of masculine/feminine qualities within a person. Anything that threatens this 'balance' tends to be avoided. When feminist-inspired goddess spirituality began to intersect with more established pagan traditions in the UK, an attitude that was often expressed was that feminists were 'unbalanced' due to their prioritization of women over men.[3]

In 1978 for example, a furor of sorts arose when at speaker at that year's Quest Conference admitted that she would consider admitting homosexuals into her magical group. Shortly afterwards, the following statement appeared in *Aquarian Arrow* magazine:

> *"Two members of the [Hornsey] group attended the 'Aquarian Age' symposium held in London on May 13th [1978]. During this meeting it was publicly stated by the leader of one group that she approved of working publicly with homosexu-*

---

[3] See Feraro, 2020, for a thorough exploration of the tensions between radical and goddess feminists and established Pagan traditions, in particular, Wicca.

*als. The [Hornsey] group wishes to dissociate itself from such
a viewpoint.*

*Further, it considers that any genuinely contacted frater-
nity could not countenance working with sexual deviants of
any sort. The reasons for this should be plain to any properly
trained occultist. It is reasonable to conclude, therefore, that of
the other 'leaders' and delegates present, there were none who
were genuinely contacted on to the Western Mysteries.* "[4]

Such a hissy fit! The outrage of the authors of the statement is palpable. They condemn an entire event and all those who attended it as
not being "genuinely contacted." Meaning that none of those present
had established the proper contact with the inner planes 'Masters'
who direct all genuine students of the Western Mystery tradition.

Gradually though, there was a shift in these attitudes across the
1980s–90s. British Wiccan authors for example, had to accommodate the increasing popularity of all same-sex covens that were becoming a more prominent feature of U.S. Wicca. Early disapproval[5] gave
way to cautious acceptance. Janet and Stewart Farrar, in their *A
Witches' Bible* (1984), noting the existence of single-sex covens, gave
their opinion that all-women covens could work, as the "cyclic
natures" of their members would provide the required "creative
polarity," but they went on to say that, in their opinion, all male-
groups would be "a mistake" and that male-only groups would be

---

[4] Quoted from Luhrmann, 1989.

[5] John Score, founding editor of *The Wiccan* (journal of the *Pagan Front*, later
the *Pagan Federation)*, was opposed to including homosexuals in the craft. In a
1970 letter to Leo Martello, for example, he stated that "no single male should
be initiated without good evidence of heterosexual attainment," and that a coven
that included homosexuals or lesbians was an "abomination." See Feraro, 2020,
p208.

best sticking to ritual magic, for example, the system of the Golden Dawn.

They go on to remark: "We deliberately refrain from commenting on the 'gay' covens (another particularly American phenomenon), because we feel that we are not equipped to do so, and because anything we could say might be interpreted as anti-homosexual prejudice." After stating that they have homosexual friends and have defended them, they go on to remark, "We have even had one or two homosexual members during our coven's history, when they have been prepared and able to assume the role of their actual gender while in a Wiccan context."[6] To give them their due, the Farrars did, over time, shift their attitudes, and in later books, openly advocated that gay men should be allowed to practice witchcraft.

At least some of the homophobic attitudes within Wicca are widely believed to stem from Gerald Gardner. Doreen Valiente, in her 1989 book, *The Rebirth of Witchcraft*, remarked that she had been told that homosexuality was "abhorrent to the Goddess," and that the Goddess would curse same-sex practitioners. Valiente says that she believed this, but later came to question it—"Why should people be 'abhorrent to the Goddess' for being born the way they are?"[7]

Yet at the same time that attitudes were changing, queers were still, by and large, expected to accommodate themselves to the male-female polarity structure to which many covens and magical groups still held fast. Thus, a gay man became 'acceptable' if he was willing to play the role of a (presumably) heterosexual male deity in dynamic tension with a goddess, probably being embodied by a straight

---

[6] Farrar, Janet & Stewart. 1984. pp169–70.
[7] Valiente, Doreen. 1989, p183.

woman. The notion that two or more gods or goddesses might want to get it on was still anathema. Further, the idea that a man might want to invoke a goddess upon themselves, or a woman a god, was still thought of as unorthodox or even 'risky' by some groups well into the late 1990s.[8]

A general problem with esoteric theories of sexuality and gender is that they are, all too often as I noted earlier, held to be cosmic truths or universal laws, rather than discourses that have emerged over time and in particular cultures. This is one reason why binary theories of polarity (drawing on electrical analogies or Jungian themes) are so hard for some practitioners to move away from; they are held to be universal principles operating at every level of existence from the personal to the cosmic. Also, works that are considered to be 'classics' of their time (such as Dion Fortune's *Psychic Self-Defence*) continue to be in circulation, effectively ensuring that the attitudes to sexuality and gender expressed by earlier generations of authors never quite lose their traction or go entirely out of fashion.

Where are we now?

Since the beginning of the new century, there has been a steady stream of books emerging that in one way or another, 'queer' magical practice or open up space for non-heterosexual practitioners who, not that long ago, would not have been even deemed capable of practising occult traditions. Some voices have accommodated to polarity discourse, bending it in the process. Some reject it utterly. These books speak to new generations of practitioners who are more aware of, and critical of the prejudices of what has gone before. The conservatism, casual racism, and universalism are glaringly obvious and are

---

[8] Greenwood, 2000, p164.

being called out as such. The idea that esoteric practice demands political and ethical commitments is no longer thought to be radical. Existing 'traditions' have been re-oriented, and new ones brought into being. Queer voices are reshaping wider occult discourse in surprising and novel ways. In many ways, we have moved from the margins to the centre. To the heart, if you like. The circle has been 'kinked.'

But the biggest change has been undoubtedly the internet, and the rise of social media. The internet has changed everything. Yes, it has its problems. I am not some rose-tinted net romantic. But the simple fact of being able to connect with another person halfway across the planet is momentous. We find that we are not alone; that communities exist; that we can create and shape communities. We can find strength in diversity, and at the same time honour difference. We can afford to be gentle, and recognise the power of collective anger. We can come together—in all the ways that that implies. It is this sense of community, of shared hope that will, I believe, sustain us in resisting those who would see us banished to the margins again.

Sources for Introduction and Prologue

Farrar, Janet & Stewart. 1984. *A Witches' Bible: The Complete Witches' Handbook.* Phoenix Publishing Inc.

Feraro, Shai. 2020. *Women and Gender Issues in British Paganism, 1945–1990.* Palgrave Macmillan.

Greenwood, Susan. 2000. *Magic, Witchcraft and the Otherworld: An Anthropology.* Berg.

bell hooks. 1984. *Feminist Theory: From Margin to Center.* South End Press.

Luhrmann, Tanya M. 1989. *Persuasions of the Witches' Craft: Ritual Magic in Contemporary England.* Harvard University Press.

Valiente, Doreen. 1989. *The Rebirth of Witchcraft.* Robert Hale.

Queer Pagan Camp:
Fly Away Big Black Crows[1]
by Lou Hart

*L*aughter could be heard across the field...a field of black silhou-
ettes made up of tents of many shapes and sizes, with small
fires glowing nearby and further away, and groups of people
sitting around them. There were lanterns hanging in the dark against
a sky bright with a full moon. The wind rose and soughed in the oak
trees and the hedgerows. Then all was still and calm on this warm
night, punctuated by faint laughter, which could be heard from all
corners of the field.

This was Queer Pagan Camp in the sixth year. It was 2003 and there
was a drought on so we had to be very careful with fire and water. We
camped that night in the same beautiful field in Dorset that we had
camped in since the first camp in 1998. It had not been ploughed in over
100 years and the owner was also a guardian of the land—leaving it
mostly wild, so rare species of plant grew there, such as the corky-
fruited water drop wort.

We didn't know then that we would be losing this beautiful place
or that there would be arguments and disagreements about QPC's
direction.

---

[1] The title of a song by Seldiy Bate often sung at QPC.

These are my best memories of Queer Pagan Camp—the laughter...oh and the creativity. At the first camp our café failed to materialize, so I asked the owner if we could use her stone barn and she agreed. Trips to the nearby recycling centre and supermarket furnished us with trestles and a counter made out of a door. Outside we fixed up an old sink for washing up; our shower was an agricultural hose running down to a corner of the field with a wooden platform where people could be heard shrieking during the hot sunshine as they went under the cold water. Everything used in the shower had to be biodegradable, and there were compost loos in the field.

There was an old cooker in the barn and some wooden seating. We bought a gas bottle and used camping stoves. We scrounged some tables for people to eat at both inside and out, and there was a mezzanine with old sofas on it where people would hang out or sometimes sleep in the evening.

Then the magic happened—nets and curtains went up, fairy lights and decorations, including small glasses of wild flowers on each table. Wall hangings were put up, and our cooks and servers wore minidresses and wellies, crowns and *bustières,* dressed as country wenches or in leathers with caps, three piece-suits and Elvis sideburns. At one point during the day, walkers on the public footpath that ran through the field (hardly ever used), came to the barn and ordered a cream tea from one of the cooks who (I think) was dressed as Raquel Welch in *10,000 Years BC.* In the nearby town we were famous for visiting the charity shops. We once overheard a conversation about "Cinderella and a Pink Mohican that had called in that day."

Everyone dressed up—and helped dress each other up. It was common to see a line of tiaraed people queuing for food in the café, and I remember once seeing two women in ball gowns, huge boots and wigs dancing around the remains of the smoky central fire in the rain. On another famous rainy day, lesbians who had never worn make-up were made up in the barn by gay men who had.

The people who came to Queer Pagan Camp were varied. They came from a variety of backgrounds: from anarchist groups, from lesbian groups, from hunt saboteurs[2], to witchcraft covens and Goddess groups, people who read tea leaves and people who worked shamanically, and those who were psychics. Basically, anyone who was pagan or interested in paganism and anyone who identified as Queer or didn't believe there was a 'norm' was welcome and especially bisexual, gay, lesbian and trans people because most of us who had been interested in spirituality or magic, pagan traditions and witchcraft had been rejected by a hetero-normative, binary-gendered world.

Social media was a bit unheard of then so we sent out a photocopied invitation (4 to a sheet) and asked the people we knew to photocopy it again, cut it up and put it in their local bookshops, pagan places and queer places. Two of us were interviewed by the *Pink Paper,* and we put articles in *Pagan Dawn* and other magazines. Our invitation was for walking the maze, chanting and singing, magic, rituals, wonky wands, and bent bollines—and if that appealed, you were welcomed.

On the first day of the first camp in 1998, we went round putting up photocopied pumpkin signs with arrows pointing in the right direction to access the field in the middle of the countryside where camp was to be held. Four of us were bent double with lump hammers, trying to put up the marquee with their super-fit owner—who wielded a sledge hammer like Wayland Smith. Fifty-eight people turned up.

---

[2] Visit huntsabs.org.uk for more information about Hunt Saboteurs and their activities & history.

Our days at camp were spent creating rituals or running workshops together—and sometimes just rope skipping in the main marquee or listening to stories in the wild area. From the start we decided we didn't want paid teachers but more of a 'be your own celebrant' approach. So, in the morning meetings people might volunteer to run a ritual and ask if anyone else would like to help. Groups of people formed to investigate elements, or divination, to drum for & run trance dances—and the soon to follow 'Prance dances' which were highly popular—with some people in fishnets and thigh length, patent leather boots. (You know who you are.)

Rituals included drawing down the moon, ritual for the animal victims of the foot and mouth epidemic, a ritual for all our ancestors who had been destroyed as witches and/or queers, a belonging ritual, a ritual where wolves were chased by hares, a masked ball, a Baphomet ritual, and many, many others. Near the end of camp there was always a cabaret with some great performances. During our live-drummed trance dances, totem animals and Spirit of the land came to dance with us, and we left an area of the field free of camping so it could be used for ritual or dreaming or to meet the Fae.

In the evening, during the first few years, after last meal, the camp sat around a huge fire and drummed, danced, told stories, sang and chanted together. We had a repertoire and many of the songs became known to us all. For me the bliss of this moment was when people started to harmonise and it became completely new and different each time.

Queer Pagan Camp operated on a sliding scale so that those on benefits could come and people on high incomes subsidised the camp. Some wanted a Play space—something those of us who liaised with the Owner/Guardian weren't sure would go down well, but it was fine. In the end, she was one of us.

There were challenges too. Some of the witches were used to working with Mother Goddesses or Kings or Queens of Fairy (which did
not go down well initially with the Anarchist contingent); some of the
gay men didn't seem to understand ageism, and there wasn't really any
childcare (although it was recognised that enabling disabled people
and women with children to come was important and the organisers
tried to ensure no-one would be turned away for lack of funds). We
also had incidents where we had to throw people off camp. In addition, we were used to being outsiders—I know for me, at the beginning, it was very hard to feel that I belonged.

So how did it come to be?

Some of us had read works by Foucault, Judith Butler, David
Halperin, Edward Carpenter, and Lucy Irigaray amongst others;
some us had been involved in establishing magical working groups or
pagan newsletters based on alternative sexualities or on other pagan
practices, such as chaos magic. A feature for me in magical working
was the idea of transgression—that our momentum took us neither
forwards nor backwards but sideways. Queer Pagan Camp actually
arose out of synchronicity. Two people I knew went to a 'Spirit' camp
where they were told they could not be spiritual because they were
not heterosexual or procreative. At the same time, I had been to a
largely heterosexual witch camp, and talked with my friend Phil afterwards (we were in a different group together) about setting something
up for Queer Witches.

Word went out and a meeting was set up. We invited queer and
pagan friends, and we were all from covens or shamanic type, animist
or other magical groups.

This was at a meeting in 1997, at which a fair few people attended,
and some continued to attend for a while or provided contacts (such

as the Guardian/Owner). We all talked about the dismissal of queer people in traditional pagan circles and the lack of awareness of the power of this rejection within organisations like the *Pagan Federation*.

Eventually there were three of us left at the meetings (all witches), and we utilized the contacts we had to secure a site. We invited one of the people—who used to attend the meetings—to set up a café which they could run at a small profit, and secured a 40′ marquee and a 20′ marquee at cost price from someone who wanted to support us. Two of us floated the camp with non-returnable donations, and Phil provided us with a 'zine documenting the rejection of queers made by well-known magical authors, New Agers, and even practitioners of yoga.

We made a decision right at the start to advertise the camp as Queer Pagan Camp because we had three areas of interest: we thought it important that it was for people who identified as Queer; who were pagan or interested in paganism; and we wanted to 'Queer-up paganism'—because our type of paganism was different from what was out there. We produced a fanzine called *The Pink Pumpkin* which ran for a few years.

We 'queered up' the magic—men carried Goddesses, women carried Gods—there were non-gendered beings or bi-gendered beings, or at one point, a multiplicity of beings (legion!) in possession. Some people didn't work with deities at all. Some of the workshops investigated inner power or explored shape-shifting. There were sound bathing workshops & Qi Gong and a labyrinth to walk. Every magical or spiritual practice was open to challenge and was sometimes changed or inverted.

The other main stipulation for Queer Pagan Camp was self-identification. This was difficult for some people who came at the beginning and did not respect trans people or bisexual people in particular, but they tended not to come back. We also got enquiries from guys who seemed to think the camp must be just about sexual kink—and although consensual kink was there and was celebrated, it was a part of camp and not the whole.

Most of the time it seemed to work, and so people broke out of their external reality affinity groups and into different affinities where we could celebrate with people that we might not otherwise have spent time with. For many of us it was a sort of coming home—to a world where we celebrated our differences and our connections with the land, with spirits, with animals, and with magic. It ran as a gift economy where people offered things from a spirit of love and generosity.

This is, of course, my recollection. Other Queer Folks may disagree and that's OK, too.

Later there were rows and arguments, people feeling betrayed and hurt over a variety of topics. Alliances were formed and broken, and somehow it was worse because we were so close at the beginning. Some people were, and still are, very, very hurt but QPC may not be finished yet...

So back to that warm night in 2003. It is late—some people have gone to bed, and the evening of drumming and singing around the main fire together has been over for quite a while. I breathe in the smell of wood smoke from the smaller fires and watch people bidding each other 'Good Night.' Some will stay up until dawn, and the laughter is even fainter now. The fireflies are glowing green in the long grass, and the moon hangs huge in the sky. It is time to rest. I know that I am where I should be.

Lou Hart is a genderqueer artist, musician & activist. They are one of the people who set up Queer Pagan Camp in the UK. She has been a wildlife artist and studied environmental literature and landscape. In an earlier time, they dabbled in ritual magic and shamanic techniques and were initiated in two non-Wiccan traditions of witchcraft. She has been active in the women's and queer rights movements for a long time. Currently working with Santa Muerte and images of the dead, they occasionally teach ritual technique.

One:
Queerying
Paganisms

I have always, regardless of whatever practice or 'tradition' I have been primarily engaged with, thought of myself as 'Pagan'. Its very fluidity—the way it can stretch to encompass myriad possibilities of lifestyle and orientation—have always seemed to me to be a strength rather than a weakness. Like 'queer,' it has many shades and interpretations. It is an acknowledgement of infinite variety and difference. Like 'queer,' it too has been used as a term of derision or disparagement. I can live with that.

Queerying Paganisms is a selection of short essays in which I explore various facets of the emerging idea of 'Queer Paganism.' They range from moments of reflection, to satire and literary criticism. I pose questions. How might a queer ethical relation reorient how we relate to deities? What, for Queer Pagans, might constitute a mystery? My approach to 'Queerying Paganisms' tries to steer clear of prescriptive statements. My intention is not to define what it means to queer paganisms, nor to nail either 'queer' or 'pagan' down into an easily-assimilated set of propositions or beliefs. Rather, I take delight in exploring the cracks and edges. To question received wisdoms and circulating narratives, especially the ones that cluster around the edges of queer paganism itself. I think of 'queer paganism' as a rather tenuous work in progress. Never complete, always open. A fuzzy shape that emerges from shadow to join the fun wherever queers come out and frolic.

The two essays on Pan in this section are part of a side project I began in 2011 with the intention of examining how Pan makes his presence felt in various historical moments, and in art and literature (amongst other things). Not infrequently Pan leaves in his wake a very queer unsettling of the normal. It is a project I will return to in the future. In the meantime, Io Pan!

1
"Knowledge Trembling in Secret"

S ometimes a phrase just jumps out at me, leaping off the page/ screen, out of the conversation and hangs there; an invitation for an adventure. I was reading Patricia MacCormack's notes after her second lecture at Treadwell's Bookshop (10th January 2010) "Pacting and Desirous Demonology" and this phrase—*knowledge trembling in secret*—lunged at me and sent me spinning into a delirium, so that I immediately began to tremble. This is a good sign for me. When my writing really starts going well, I often experience this 'trembling,' and in a way, my writing emerges from this. Trembling from unfocused excitement, desire—a profound disturbance of equilibrium, like the shivering of a racehorse before the starting gun. It can be overwhelming at times and can go on for days, disrupting my sleep patterns. I often think of it as 'tipping' me into something. Trembling is, of course, a sign of possession and there's a lot about 'trembling' as a sign in tantric texts. There's a whole set of relations in tantra among yoga, possession, sovereignty and power/achievement which I think hasn't made it out of academia.

The immediate resonance was that of knowledge as corporeal—a bodily state rather than an abstraction divorced from the flesh.

Then there's secrecy. I've been thinking a lot about secrecy recently—mostly in terms of Bourdieu's notion of cultural capital, but again, this phrasing brings to mind the idea of secrets which can only be known through the body and relational encounters with other bodies. Secrecy arising out of communion—the sharing of moments which cannot be abstracted, codified, recorded. There's an idea in some tantric texts that at the point of initiation, the guru 'enters' the disciple's body in order to transfer *Śakti* (power, capacity). Again, there's a possession theme. There's a fascinating discussion of these themes in Gavin Flood's *The Tantric Body: The Secret Tradition of Hindu Religion* (I.B. Tauris, 2006)—particularly in relation to the *Isanasivagurudeva-paddhati* (ISG), where various groupings (packs) of beings *(bhutas, grahas,* etc.) enter the body via one's shadow. The ISG collapses the distinction between individual and that which possesses them—so a possessed person, according to the ISG, becomes a *bhuta.* Again, this highlights the ease in South Asian thought with which a human can become a deity or a spirit.

Why does "knowledge tremble in secret"?

Does knowledge tremble out of fear? Fear of being dragged out of the dark, abstracted, dissected, chained and trapped in books? Or does knowledge tremble in anticipation? The anticipation of a new lover's arrival; the longing for a tryst? It brings to mind a line in Neil Gaiman's *Sandman* story "Calliope" where Erasmus Fry says to Richard Madoc of the Muses, "One is supposed to woo them, but I've always found force to be effective."

This is a classic Kristeva scenario—the abjection of the ambiguous Calliope, who blurs the boundaries between human/divine through Madoc's act of rape, recreates him as the successful author—who nonetheless describes himself (later in the story) as a 'feminist.' She, on the other hand, is reduced to the spectre in the locked room— Madoc's 'guilty secret.' Only *he* is real, only *he* is a subject, whilst

Calliope is thoroughly objectified—merely an emptied vessel into which Madoc pours his seed and takes, takes, takes. The violence of this act is heightened by the suggestion that Calliope is child-like. She is the virgin who produces the word. I'm reminded of some of the early twentieth-century works on 'sexual magic' where women are merely 'vessels' for the creations of the male magus—distant, symbolically-ordered presences of spiritual/occult projection and objectification. Idealised goddess-women who 'promise' sex and power, but cannot be allowed to own their own agency and sexuality. Be what we want you to be, or we'll hurt you; cast you out, seems to be the message.

2

Pan: "Disreputable Objects of Pagan Licentiousness"

"Shocking things go on here. You wouldn't believe it! Licentiousness! Orgies! ... Even bingo. Oh yes."
— Lurcio (Frankie Howerd), *Up Pompeii*

"If a boy has the fortune to be born beautiful, but does not offer his arse for the enjoyment of others, may he fall in love with a beautiful girl and never manage to bed her."
— Graffiti found at Pompeii

I n 1734, Charles of Bourbon, king of Naples and Sicily commenced a programme of digging around Naples to search for classical treasures, which led to the excavation of Herculaneum, the rediscovery of Pompeii (in 1763), and the Villa dei Papiri. The discoveries—which included the Villa of Diomedes (1771) in which were found the bodies of women and children caught by the eruption—attracted great interest. By the 1760s Naples and Pompeii had become one of the favourite stopping points for those undertaking the Grand Tour. But amidst the wealth of classical treasures brought out of the ground, were objects of a more troubling nature. One such find was a marble statue of Pan copulating with a goat, unearthed from the Villa dei Papiri in 1752, in the presence of Charles, his wife, and his courtiers.

Charles was shocked by this find, ordered the excavations to be halted, and consigned the statue to a cupboard, with access granted only with the direct permission of the king himself. Johann Winckelmann asked permission to view the statue, but was turned down. Standards must have lapsed later, as Richard Payne Knight, in his *Discourse on the Worship of Priapus* (1786) refers to the statue as 'well-known.' In the early nineteenth century, this statue became part of the collection of the so-called "Secret Cabinet" to which access was restricted to only "persons of mature age and of proven morality," a decree made by Francis I in 1819, after visiting the Royal Bourbon Museum. By 1823, any artefacts judged to be "disreputable objects of pagan licentiousness" were restricted to this private room.

One N. Brooke, in his *Observations on the manners and customs of Italy* (1798), was apparently so disturbed by the sculpture of Pan and the goat that he reported it to be made of bronze, rather than marble.

News of these discoveries travelled quickly, despite Bourbon attempts to restrict publications relating to the excavations. The diplomat, Dominique-Vivant Denon, made a series of drawings (including the infamous Pan & goat) based on the erotic artefacts from Pompeii, and published it under the title *Priapees et sujets divers.* Collectors converged on Naples, and there was a brisk trade in manufactured copies of erotic objects. Johann Winckelmann reported finding on the market forgeries of Priapic figures from Pompeii in paint and sculpture. One venetian artist, Guiseppe Guerra, specialised in producing copies of frescoes dominated by phallic images, for sale to enthusiastic tourists.

Pierre-Sylvain Maréchal, between 1780 and 1803, published a nine-volume work devoted to the finds at Herculaneum, which contained engravings of Priapean themes (though Pan was omitted). Maréchal, whilst portraying the ancient Romans as 'childlike' and 'innocent' tended to apologise for the presence of erotic imagery and artefacts.

Before the excavations at Pompeii and Herculaneum, Rome had been thought as a font of austere majesty and wisdom, but as the excavations uncovered a wide range of sexually explicit objects and scenes—painted on walls and floor mosaics, on vases, in sculpture and everyday objects—scholars gradually (and reluctantly) concluded that such erotic displays were not exceptions, but the rule. One popular notion which arose in the wake of these discoveries was that the Roman Empire had collapsed because of moral corruption and depravity.

There is considerable evidence to suggest that literate people in the eighteenth century were aware of ancient Greek and Roman sexual behaviour. References to ancient same-sex lovers such as Ganymede and Antinous appear throughout eighteenth-century texts both as terms of derision and 'codes' for establishing shared interest. Anne Lister, for example, is said to have learned Latin and Greek in order to seek out references to love and sex between women, and also used classical references to same-sex love in negotiating her affairs with other women. Petronius' infamous Roman novel, *Satyricon* was available in the eighteenth century, and there is a reference made to its 'sodomitical' influence in Tobias Smollett's (1748) novel, *The Adventures of Roderick Random*.

The Grand Tour

In the eighteenth century it became fashionable for young men of wealth and rank to go on "the Grand Tour" to France and Italy in order to have their education polished. The Tour generally lasted between two and five years, and the great cultural centres of Paris, Rome and Naples were favourite stopping points. The discoveries at

Pompeii and Herculaneum also added to the attractions of the Grand Tour, and wealthy antiquarians flocked to Naples, first as collectors, and later as dealers. Sir William Hamilton, the British envoy to Naples from 1764, amassed an enormous collection of antiquities, and his residence became a popular stop on the Tour. The Tour was also an opportunity for sexual adventure, and there were frequent worries that travel to France and Italy would 'effeminate' young men. Italy, in particular, had a reputation for sodomy and tracts such as *Reasons for the Growth of Sodomy in England* (1729) blamed Italian influences such as opera, whilst Churchill's 1764 poem *The Times* had it that:

> *"ITALIA, nurse of ev'ry softer art,*
> *Who, feigning to refine, unmans the heart,*
> *Who lays the realms of Sense and Virtue waste,*
> *Who marrs whilst she pretends to mend our taste,*
> *ITALIA, to compleat and crown our shame."*[1]

Attitudes to Italy were also coloured by anti-Catholic sentiments, and by the climatic theory of temperament. For example, Montesquieu, in his 1748 work, *The Spirit of the Laws* claimed that people of cold climates tended to be industrious and orderly, whilst those who dwelt in hot climates tended to be lazy and chaotic.

In addition to its cultural possibilities, the Grand Tour was also attractive for the possibility of sexual adventures—including those of

---

[1] Rictor Norton (Ed.), "The Times by Charles Churchill, 1764", *Homosexuality in Eighteenth-Century England: A Sourcebook*. Updated 1 Dec. 1999 <http://rictornorton.co.uk/eighteen/1764chur.htm>.

a transgressive nature. William Beckford referred to Italy as "the place for sinners of a certain sort."[2]

The discoveries at Pompeii and Herculaneum also helped fuel a rise in interest in Classical art—and collections of classical art became emblems of the wealth and taste of their owners. Such was the passion of English collectors for examples of classical art that one contemporary Italian commented, "Were our Amphitheatre portable, the English would carry it off." Not only was the acquisition and possession of art a form of social prestige, but also it was considered desirable to display at the very least an articulate enthusiasm for one's collection. This led to the growth of interest in theories of art.

The collections of antiquarians such as Elias Ashmole, Charles Townley, Richard Payne Knight, and Sir William Hamilton contributed heavily to the foundation of the British Museum. Charles Townley (1737–1805), possessed a terracotta reproduction of Pan and the she-goat by the English sculptor, Joseph Nollekens, who had viewed the original in the 1760s (it ended up in the British Museum's "Private Case" which later, in 1865, became known as the "Secret Museum"). This also led to a re-evaluation of myth. Early Enlightenment thought tended not to admire myth—rationalists such as Voltaire and David Hume portrayed myth as an erroneous attempt by primitive people to explain the world, and deists such as John Toland saw both Christianity and pagan myth as corruptions of a

---

[2] Beckford (1760–1844) was a novelist most remembered for his gothic fantasy "Vathek". In 1784 he left England, together with his wife, when his affair with the young William Courtney (later 9th Earl of Devon) was discovered, and the newspapers circulated rumours about Beckford and his "Kitty" (Courtney). See Rictor Norton, "William Beckford: The Fool of Fonthill", *Gay History and Literature,* updated 16 Nov. 1999
<http://www.rictornorton.co.uk/beckfor1.htm>

natural primitive monotheism. The discoveries at Pompeii and Herculaneum led to a new interest in interpreting myths as a necessary part of the Classical past.

One influential theorist of ancient art—who also contributed to the rise of interest in Roman erotic themes (particularly the popular notion of 'Roman Orgies')—was the self-styled Baron d'Hancarville (1719–1805) who was engaged by Sir William Hamilton to produce a sumptuous catalogue of his collection—a four-volume set of illustrated volumes, accompanied by an essay on the origins of Greek art. (Hamilton's catalogue of vases was an influence on James Wedgwood, who began to produce vases based on the illustrations of Hamilton's collection in his pottery factory.)

d'Hancarville was by all accounts a colourful character, an art historian who supplanted his income with occasional theft and the production of pornographic works. Around 1769–1770, d'Hancarville produced two pornographic works. One was *Monumens de la vie privee des douze Cesars* ("Monuments of the private lives of the twelve Caesars") which purported to be a catalogue of etchings taken from various antique objects that depicted the sexual adventures of the various Roman emperors; but the etchings were 'fictional,' being drawn from the works of Suetonius and Tacitus. (Vivant Denon may have been one of the engravers who produced the illustrations.) d'Hancarville also authored *Monumens du culte secret des Dames Romaines* ("Monuments of the secret rites of Roman Women") which again purported to show illustrations drawn from cameos depicting pagan erotic practices. *Caesars* was scandalous, but also proved to be popular—and pirated editions began to circulate.

d'Hancarville went on to publish *Recherches sur l'Origine, l'Esprit les Progres des Arts de la Grece* (1785), a central theme of which was that all art in every culture originated from a single primitive religion, and that this religion was sexual in nature. He attempted to demonstrate that that the image of a bull breaking an egg (the bull representing the generative power of the creator) can be found in every culture. d'Hancarville proposed that previous interpretations of the mythology of the Classic world, which relied on texts, were incorrect. Instead, he concentrated on the artefacts being revealed at Pompeii— vases, sculptures, coins and engraved gems. d'Hancarville, Hamilton (and Charles Townley) played a role in the publication of Richard Payne Knight's *A Discourse on the Worship of Priapus* (1786).

The sculpture of Pan and the goat now resides in the "Gabinetto Segreto" ("Secret Chamber") section of Naples' National Archeological Museum, together with a statue of a rather lecherous Pan together with Daphnis, which was originally part of the Farnese collection. The collection was made viewable by the general public in 2000.

3

Queer Pagans or
Queering Paganisms?

I've been involved in the UK Queer Pagan scene for a number of years now, but whenever I decide to try to write about this, I find myself reflecting on what for me is a core issue: what happens when *Queer* is placed next to *Pagan*? It strikes me that there are two ways—related but divergent—in which the phrase 'Queer Pagan' can be thought through. Firstly, as a noun, 'Queer Pagan' can be read as an umbrella term, encompassing a multitude of identity-positions where perhaps the only commonality is varying degrees of commitment to refusing/resisting the heteronormative gender binary. However, it's the second usage of 'Queer Pagan' which I want to focus on for now, where 'queer' is a verb, signifying a radical process of disruption—where the focus shifts from Queer Pagan as an identity-position towards *Queering-Paganism* as process.

What does can it mean to 'queer' something? Queering can be thought of a process of disrupting, disturbing and questioning the normal—that which is 'taken-for-granted.' Queer sidles up to identities, ideologies; any category that has been taken to be timeless, solid and foundational, and exposes gaps, fissures, resistances, instabilities, different possibilities, and surprises. As Jeffrey J. Cohen says in *Medieval Identity Machines,* "Queering is at its heart a process of wonder." I want that on a T-shirt.

Part of this commitment to challenge, uncover the hidden, look backstage and discover how productions are produced, is the commitment to keep 'queer' fuzzy and indeterminant. It is a recognition of the importance of not slipping back into an 'us-them' binary which privileges a heroic 'transgressive' queer subject against those still bound up in normative relations.

Someone asked me recently if Queer Paganism could be thought of as a 'tradition.' It begs a questioning of how the very concept of 'Traditions' is used in Pagan discourse. 'Tradition' is sometimes used to denote a commonality of praxis—which is to say that it often implies common practices, ideologies, political alliances—and often there is an implication that this praxis is historically located, a kind of sense that what we do now was done by our ancestors, sort of thing. Tradition can be thought of (simplifying hugely) as an appeal to unity to varying degrees, and can act as a boundary in making distinctions between one approach to praxis and another. But for Queer Pagan(ism), such appeals to unity can only be, I think, of a temporary nature. One thing I see as central to Queer Paganism is a commitment to diversity and difference, which involves allowing a place for dissent, and the understanding that dissent is itself productive, rather than a failure. Equally, making a case for a historical Queer Paganism is also tricky—although we can talk (at length!) about celebrating queer ancestors, reading queerness into and out of histories, of uncovering the politics of dissent hidden behind monolithic accounts of the past. I don't think that's quite the same as rooting a Queer Pagan praxis in the deep, undifferentiated past, if only because I tend to think of Queer Paganism as something new; queer theory and queer activism both emerged out of the 1990s. If one can speak of 'Queer Pagan Tradition' at all, then it is as something that is relational to particular alliances and networks, produced within and temporary to heterotopic spaces such as the UK's *Queer Pagan Camp (QPC)*. Perhaps a sense of shared tradition emerges when Queer Pagans come together to laugh, celebrate, dance and argue, but outside of such spaces it recedes, dissolving like morning dew. I'd suggest that, rather than looking at tradition as a boundary which encloses particular practices (such as theologies, rituals, etc.), what seems to me to be of more concern within a Queer Pagan space is a commitment to an ethic of mutual care and reciprocity; to an invitation to play with boundaries and categories; to celebrate difference. It's this ethical openness—primarily towards sexual and gender—but also other forms of difference which I see as central to understanding Queer Pagan approaches; that queer need not be an either/or choice made in opposition to other identities, but (depending on context/ situation) possibly a 'both/and' choice, or even a 'neither/nor' choice. Opening to the possibilities of fluidity entails an acceptancy of multiple orientations and positions that shift according to particular contexts and situations.

If this is a tradition (in a loose sense), it's one that is being passed around, rather than handed down. It's focused towards what might be thought of as *a politics of doing* rather than a mode of being.

This, for me, is related to queer theory's attention to the exposure, and challenging of how subjects are produced through binary identity categories: heteronormative ideologies, practices, values and assumptions. At the same time, queer theories have contributed to the perspective that identities (including, but not limited to sexual identities) can be thought of as fluid and changing—where selfhood (the "I" position) is not generated in opposition to an *other*, but discursively negotiated *through* others. Similarly, activist groups such as *Queeruption* have stressed the importance of non-separationist politics: for example, fuzzying the boundary between serious political work and frivolous personal play, and attempting to break down the boundaries between 'leaders' and 'the led.' At QPC for instance, anyone can turn up and offer a workshop, a discussion, a public ritual, but this is done on the basis of sharing—workshop facilitators are not paid, nor are they accorded the status which at other events, tends to reinforce a distinction between leaders and consumers.

So, back to Queering-Paganism, something which may take the form of Wicca with added glitter, or ceremonial magic in high heels, but also examining/critiquing various strands of Pagan discourse from different queer perspectives. Thus far such examinations have tended to focus on the ways in which Pagan discourses of sexuality & gender uphold the logic of the heteronormative gender binary in both practices and metaphysics. In America, there are signs that the controversy sparked by the exclusion of transgendered Pagans at *Pantheacon*[1] in 2012 is also provoking a closer critique of Pagan discourses around sexuality and gender—and despite the surface rhetoric of being 'inclusive,' how Pagan praxis actually works against this, producing separations and boundaries. I see these projects as the *beginnings* of conversations that I hope will spiral outwards into wider areas—asking provocative questions and opening up new possibilities for exploration.

With thanks to Gavin Brown for some provocative writing and conversation.

---

[1] See Essay 15, footnote 1, for a brief summary of this event.

4

Cross Bones: Queering Sacred Space?

Whenever I exit London Bridge station, I make a brief nod in the direction of Cross Bones graveyard—it is part of my recognition of London's network of sacred spaces. I've been to some of the monthly vigils held at this site, but more often than not, just strolling past it and knowing that it's there amid the bustle of London is enough for me. A couple of mornings ago, I wandered down to the gate and spent a few minutes gazing at it, occasionally reaching out to briefly touch the ribbons, some inscribed with names and dates from the eighteenth century, festooning the bars. A van passes, a train slowly clunks across the bridge over Redcross Way. Reflecting on what this materialisation of death and loss meant for me, whilst stroking a faded ribbon, brought to mind Carolyn Dinshaw's evocative phrase from her book, *Getting Medieval,* of the need for making "a touch across time."

Cross Bones graveyard was 'discovered' in the 1990s by the *Museum of London Archaeology Service* during the construction of the Jubilee Underground line. In 1992, 148 skeletons were removed, and the archaeologists estimated that the site could contain up to 15,000 bodies. Cross Bones has been identified as an unconsecrated graveyard, primarily used to inter prostitutes who were excluded from Christian burial.

61

Cross Bones is part of the "Southwark Stews". In the fourteenth century, Southwark came under the jurisdiction of the City of London, but certain areas, called 'liberties' remained under the control of powerful church officials. It was in the so-called Liberty of Winchester (controlled by the Bishop Winchester), that the 'stews'— licensed brothels—were established. (The name 'stews' comes from the vapour baths by which brothel-goers tried to steam themselves free of venereal disease.) It's likely that Southwark had a thriving brothel culture before the enterprising bishop decided to profit from legalising and regulating them. The area was renowned for a variety of 'noisome' trades, such as brewing, tanning and lime-burning, as well as small traders who wanted to escape the craft and guild regulations of the City. Southwark was also home to a large proportion of foreigners described using the term *Doche* (which encompassed Dutch, Flemish and Germans). The ordinances drawn up to regulate the brothels included the strictures that prostitutes were barred from living or boarding at the stewhouses, and during religious holidays the prostitutes had to leave not only the stewhouses, but the entire area of the liberty (both these regulations were routinely violated of course), and the stewhouses were ordered closed during nights when Parliament sat. Women who took lovers and maintained them financially were punished with prison (the bishop had his own prison, the Clink), fines and banishment from the area. Once a woman became 'public property' she had no right to a private life. It is from these regulations that the euphemism 'single women' (used to describe Cross Bones) emerges with the attendant idea that women who were not attached to a husband were, in effect, common property. Whilst the City of London had no legal jurisdiction over Southwark, its councilors attempted to keep prostitutes from the Stews out of the city. For example, in 1351, prostitutes were barred from adopting the dress of "good and noble dames" (vestments trimmed with fur or lined with silk), and told to wear only simple clothes and a striped hood; and an order in 1391 banned boatmen from ferrying men and women across the river to the stews.

In the eighteenth century, Cross Bones had become a general graveyard for paupers, and by 1853 the site was apparently so full of bodies that it was closed as a health hazard, and for the most part, forgotten, until its rediscovery in the 1990s.

Why then, choose Cross Bones for reflections on queering sacred space?

As Adrian Harris says in his paper, *'Honouring the Outcast Dead'* Cross Bones is a unique "sacred site." Its 'discovery' is fairly recent, for a start, and like many fragments of London's history, it almost seamlessly blends into the maze of architectural styles; were it not for the iron beribboned gate, it would be just another walled-off area, easy to miss, easy to walk past.

Considered as a Pagan site for finding connection with the sacred, Cross Bones is somewhat atypical; unlike more familiar sacred sites such as Stonehenge or Avebury, it is located within an urban setting. I think this itself makes Cross Bones worthy of more attention. Despite occasional forays into 'urban shamanism,' Pagan discourses on sacred sites tend to focus on sacred place-making outside of metropolitan centres. Nor can Cross Bones be easily accommodated in the 'pagan ownership' narratives that sometimes underwrite contestations of sacred space; the notion that prior to the onset of Christianity (or even the Romans) such sites were 'pagan' and that on that basis, contemporary Pagans are 'reclaiming' the space as their own. Nor is it immediately obvious how a graveyard for sex workers and infants intersects with the broader theme of 'honouring/ connecting with ancestors' via the perspective that sites such as

Avebury or Stonehenge represent ancient forms of spirituality. Again, Cross Bones is different—its sacredness is new, a product of its rediscovery and the subsequent events held there. Adrian, in his paper, draws a parallel between the tokens on the gate at Cross Bones and the "shrines" that mark "the site of road accident deaths," but they also recall for me, the 'rag tree' offerings at West Kennet, Avebury and Augustine's Well at Cerne Abbas.

At the same time, Cross Bones is a fragile site, dependent for its survival, ultimately, on the willingness of Transport for London (TfL), for whom the site represents a prime development area, to work with 'local community concerns' such as The Friends of Cross Bones' proposal that part be put aside for a memorial garden. It is also 'fragile' in the sense that it is not segregated from other spaces. It is not, for the most part, a 'quiet' space where one can easily gain that sense of hushed reverence we tend to associate with the experience of 'sacred space' (from standing stones to Christian churches).

Cross Bones is, I'd suggest, a site where pluralistic affiliations coexist and collide. You don't have to make an affiliation with John Constable's elaborate *Southwark Mysteries* to appreciate Cross Bones, or to feel a connection with the 'outcast dead' interred there. That is a matter of self-identification, and the public Cross Bones events have a firm commitment to inclusiveness—no one would be turned away for not being sufficiently 'outcast,' and the events attract a wide variety of attendees: people who live in the area, visiting Pagans, Christians, local politicians and the London Mayor. As Cross Bones events are not only celebratory, but also work to raise the profile of the site in order that it is not built over, the events have to be inclusive to the widest possible spectrum of potential allies.

Although it is well-recognised that the site is Christian (albeit 'outcast Christians'), and as Adrian points out, the only icon inside the graveyard is a statue of the Madonna, London Pagans make up a good proportion of those who attend both the monthly vigils and the Halloween festivals which have been held yearly there since 1998. More recently, Cross Bones has become incorporated into walking events organised by Cooltan Arts—marking *International Women's Day* and *International Day Against Homophobia and Transphobia*—which in 2011 included a blessing by the Sisters of Perpetual Indulgence (the *May Day Largactyl Shuffle)* at Cross Bones. Not only is Cross Bones a site for remembering its interred "Whores and Paupers of Southwark," but in 2007, messages were pinned to the gate memorialising five women sex-workers who were murdered that year in Ipswich. It has also been recognised as an important site by the International Union of Sex Workers who would like to see it preserved as a memorial for sex workers. There are other possible claimants, too. An 1833 report, expressing concerns over public health and grave-robbing, speaks of Cross Bones having an "Irish Corner."

> *"Here lay your hearts, your flowers,*
> *Your Book of Hours,*
> *Your fingers, your thumbs,*
> *Your Miss You, Mums.*
> *Here hang your hopes, your dreams, Your Might-Have-Beens,*
> *Your locks, your keys, Your Mysteries."*
> — *The Southwark Mysteries*

Cross Bones would not have become a sacred space without John Constable, whose visionary contact with a genius loci, 'the Goose' moved him to begin the monthly vigils, the celebrations, and the campaign to preserve the site in some form, assuming the magical persona of 'John Crow'. His play, *The Southwark Mysteries,* has been performed at both the Globe Theatre and Southwark Cathedral, and

caused a minor controversy when it was first performed, due to its
depictions of a 'swearing Jesus' and a female Satan wearing a strap-on
dildo. Although John Crow's own magical perspective is often the
first point of contact for people wanting to find out more about Cross
Bones, I think what is interesting here is that he works hard to stress
that what is happening at the site is an 'unfolding vision' rather than
an attempt to create a particular doctrine.

The form of the ritual embodies these contraries: combining a
sense of awe and reverence with a bawdy humour befitting the Goose.
It presents a syncretic vision of healing and transformation, rooted in
native pagan animism and John Crow's idiosyncratic Goddess worship, and encompassing elements of 'left-hand' Magdalene Gnosti-
cism, Buddhism, Tantra, spiritualism and the Western Magical Tradition. However, John Crow has always asserted that the Goose's teachings are not a doctrine, creed or belief-system. They can best be understood as a spiritual practice in which conflicting ideas can co-exist
within a state of 'Liberty' or ongoing process of liberation. The Southwark Mysteries and other teachings of the Goose/Crow source are
revealed in poetry and song, as allusions and emblems of that which
cannot be spoken, rather than as literal, 'gospel' truth.

Yet at the same time that John Crow makes this appeal to openness—to an "ongoing process of liberation"—I think it is obvious
that the events he has staged there have played an instrumental role in
shaping the emerging 'mysteries' of Cross Bones. I wonder if, in time,
other enactments will accrue around similar burial sites in London
such as Cripplegate in Warwick Place or the Bethlem graveyard (again
recently rediscovered due to excavations around Liverpool Street
Station)? Possibly only if someone comes forwards who is passionate
about the sites to devote care and attention to them.

Carolyn Dinshaw, in *Getting Medieval* describes what she terms the "queer historical impulse"—a desire to make that "touch across time" that is based not in continuity but a "shared positionality"—an "impulse toward making connections across time between, on the one hand, lives, texts, and other cultural phenomena left out of sexual categories back then and, on the other, those left out of current sexual categories now."[1]

She proposes a politics based not on identity—that is, the continuist model of history which emphasises an easy, essential sameness between past and present, but using the past, and a sense of partial connection to work for connectivity and coalition, crossing boundaries not only across time, but more conventional divides (such as academic-nonacademic, or queer-normative). Dinshaw's work seeks to interrupt the temporal separation between past and present.

Cross Bones, I think, fits well with both of these strands, in terms of its coalition, inclusive politics, and its presence as a tangible reminder that the past is never truly gone, that it continues to be felt and that its meanings are always contested, revised, and reconfigured.

In 2014, TfL granted a lease for the Bankside Open Spaces Trust (BOST) to create a 'meanwhile garden' on the site. The garden is funded by public donations and managed by volunteer wardens. Find out more at: https://crossbones.org.uk/

Sondra L. Hausner's 2016 book, *The Spirits of Crossbones Graveyard: Time, Ritual, and Sexual Commerce in London* (Indiana University Press) is an exploration of Cross Bones' tangled past and contemporary usage.

---

[1] Dinshaw, 1999, p1.

5

On Queering Deity

I've been thinking a lot recently about *Queer* as a form of resistance to identification—a refusal to be categorised or reified into some kind of essential formation. One of my objections to polarity is that, as a form of discourse, it binaries everything according to an either/or regime of signification, and can only, it seems, admit contradiction and ambiguity by having a 'third space' which still relies on the other two points, no matter how much it seems to challenge them (i.e., one gets to be male, female, a bit of both, or neither). I've taken this from something Eve Sedgwick says about queer as a resistance to the very idea of fixed gender/sexual identity as if these were natural givens or transparently empirical categories, rather than historical/cultural formations. It's about making the choice not to be limited to either this, that, or the bit in the middle: it's a celebration of diversity and complexity, contingency and contradiction.

I've been pondering recently how pagan and occult discourses tend to frame deities. A very common approach is that deities are 'biographised,' in the sense that books on magic tend to do short thumbnail biographies of deities, their appearance, likes, dislikes, maybe a myth or two in which they feature, their 'functions' (what they are 'for'), the symbolism associated with them, and often, their place in a particular pantheon—frequently with all the brevity of a *Craigslist* personal ad. This strikes me as reductive, particularly the way that deities get to be limited to particular functions ('deity **x** is a healer, deity **y** is for courage,' etc.). I think that because we are used, in Western culture, to thinking of ourselves as bounded, stable individuals possessing a fixed essence (a particular sexuality, for example), agency and limitations, that we tend to represent deities in the same way.

And by extension, it seems to me that there's a tendency to approach deities purely in terms of 'what they can do for us.' Not long ago, I was approached just prior to doing a public ritual with the question, "What lesson will Kali teach me?" I must admit I was surprised, as I've never thought of Kali as 'teaching particular lessons.' Sure, one can look back at life events and see a lesson learned (or not, as the case may be), but wanting to know a lesson in advance strikes me as peculiar. It is another kind of demand-making, and seems an odd way to begin one's relationship with a deity.

The kind of 'hard' polytheism which is getting so popular nowadays, and which tends to treat all deities as separate, individual beings, is in some ways, I think, a reflection of this tendency. It's also a response to the paganism of the 1970s–80s which tended to diffuse all deities into 'archetypes' (e.g., Pan is the same as Krishna). Both approaches have their problems; the archetypal perspective tends to ignore historical and cultural influences in favour of a universalisation of deity (all deities which share features a,b,c are instances or facets of archetype X), and the hard polytheism which makes all deities separate and individual tends to ignore situations where deities merge into one another (such as Kali becoming Krishna). Both tend to privilege 'the past' as more authoritative than the recent, and so find it difficult to accommodate 'new' deities such as AIDS-Amma or Santoshima in India. (I've been involved in many arguments about the appropriateness of worshipping Buffy as a deity, for example.) Both approaches have difficulty with contingency, contradiction and the paradoxical—the 'queerness' of deities, if you like—which resides in their protean instability—so often found in Greek narratives of desire. Look at Zeus becoming a swan for Leda, a bull for Europa, an eagle for Ganymede, and a shower of gold for Danae. That last one is particularly 'queer,' don't you think?

There's a tendency, I think, to seek in our conceptions of deity an idealised reflection of our own preferred conceptual categories, and in so doing, to lose sight of both their historical origins and contexts and, importantly, their instabilities and excesses.

Revisiting my reflections on 'queering' Baphomet[1], one of the points I was trying to get across was that we need not restrict Baphomet to the human-animal, polygendered hybrid; that the 'static' image of Baphomet (as in Eliphas Levi's depiction) can be considered but one of their many forms—a temporary 'snapshot' perhaps—but we are more than our photos, yes? We might think of the iconographical image as a partial representation, that the stillness of the form hides the seething exuberance of life exceeding all limitations, refusing to be chained by expectations and definitions, escaping limitations and overflowing any attempt to categorise and capture. One might, for example, imagine a completely non-human Baphomet— insectoid, amoeboid, a cybernet Baphometic, a Baphomet of systems in decay; a Baphomet emerging out of mucous and sticky bodily fluids; a Baphomet formed from the dreams of dead cities. So, if we're to think of Baphomet as queer in the way I've written about queer above, what does this entail? We could say, for example, that Baphomet is a representation of Queer's refusal to be defined, an orientation to the world given (temporary) form as a chimeric assemblage—a multiplicious, many-bodied hybrid which exceeds any

---

[1] See my essay, "Queering Baphomet" in *Hine's Varieties: Chaos & Beyond*, Original Falcon Press, 2019.

attempt at being defined, codified and reduced. The 'sum' of all our desires/differences known and as yet unthought. Not the capacity to be a shape-shifter, but continually shifting shape, blurring boundaries, weeds pushing through pavement cracks, the inviting smile of a stranger when you least expect it. This, I think, invites us to think about deities and our relation to them, in a different way.

6

To Baphomet, Posing as Sodomite

"No—it wasn't that way at all. It was everywhere—a gelatin—a slime—yet it had shapes, a thousand shapes of horror beyond all memory. There were eyes—and a blemish. It was the pit—the maelstrom—the ultimate abomination. Carter, it was the unnamable!"

— H.P. Lovecraft, *The Unnamable*

"He used to wonder at the shallow psychology of those who conceive the Ego in man as a thing simple, permanent, reliable and of one essence. To him, man was a being with myriad lives and myriad sensations, a complex multiform creature that bore within itself strange legacies of thought and passion, and whose flesh was tainted with the monstrous maladies of the dead."

— Oscar Wilde, *The Picture of Dorian Gray*

Prologue—pre-ritual conversation:
Q: What will happen when Baphomet comes through?
A: I don't know. It's better not to predict what might, or might not happen.
Q: But how will I know what to do?

A: That's a good question...but I don't have an answer. Why is that important?

Q: Then why are we doing this?

A: Excuse me?

Q: I mean, what's the intent?

A: There isn't one.

Q: But shouldn't we be asking for something?

A: Do you always ask someone for something when you meet them for the first time? You ask for something, and you've already set limits on what might be possible. Why not open yourself to the encounter? Let yourself be surprised...

W hen I look at Eliphas Levi's Baphomet-image, which for the most part has set the tone for artistic representations onwards (H.R. Giger and Michael Manning are two that spring to mind), I find myself thinking that despite all the yakking about androgyny—of divine hermaphrodites, of the union, of blurring, of opposites—that this image is, for the most part, masculine. More than that, it suggests a kind of hypermasculinity, a rugby player with comedy breasts. It's a solid surface, no visible openings (no mouth, no cunt, no arse). Baphomet, in this form at least, can only be a 'top'—a strutting cock-god. Which is all very well, but not necessarily 'queer' in the way that Baphomet is often held up to be.

Similarly, there is a kind of machismo—a *baphomachismo*—around Baphomet in books of magic; the idea that encountering Baphomet is risky, dangerous, challenging; a walk on the wild side; the heroic journey into the darkness. Sexy, virile, aggressive, confident, this Baphomet reifies the masculine, transgressive outsider stance beloved of occultists, which ignores issues of power and privilege, and even less how 'transgression' is bound up with contemporary self-making.

I ask an artist, "What would a Baphomet made of flowers be like?"

"What kind of flowers?"

"How about Pansies?"

"Pansy Baphomet?"

Sissy Baphomet. We all know the words (and many of us grew up with them echoing in our ears): pansy, fag, sissy, flamer, nance, *girl*, jessie, big girl's blouse, fairy, swish, queer, cry-baby, mother's-boy, wimp. It's interesting how many of these terms denote characteristics associated with femininity: weakness, passivity, vulnerability. To be judged a sissy is to be a failure of masculinity. To be a nonmale or too female—effeminate. It's a warning of a boundary about to be crossed; that there are limits and these limits, which constrain and produce the autonomous male subject, are rigorously (and aggressively) policed. The proper response being to return/share in what Robert Brandon calls "the relentless repudiation of the feminine."

Effeminacy as a condition is both achieved (lack of exercise, too much time spent with women) and innate (biological, a female soul in a man's body). In contemporary culture, effeminacy serves as a marker for same-sex interests, but it has historically been used to indicate an excessive interest in the opposite sex, too. In eighteenth-century English literature, for example, effeminacy was a charge of excessive behavior which could be directed at either women or men. It held a wide range of meanings relating to luxury, idleness, frivolity, lack of self-restraint, passion—challenges to the emerging neoliberal subjectivity.

In a previous reflection on Baphomet (*Queering Baphomet*)[1] I made the rather obvious point that Baphomet can be thought of as a monstrous body, a chimeric assemblage:

> "*an excess of signs; goat-breasted-horned-fire-winged-phallus; a surface from which multiple abjects—woman-satan-sabbat—bubble and froth. Between goat-horns blazes a fire; not the managed alchemical fire of science, more the fecund moist heat of the compost heap. Snake-entwined cock, hidden cunt. The implosion of possibilities; surfaces; sufferances. Baphomet pulses—is a pulsation of life unbound; the mystery at the heart of the sabbat; a blurred image at the edge of the firelight; an offering to the unspeakable.*"

In Baphomet though, beyond the blurring of the distinction between beast/human, god/man, demon/man, woman/man, there is a very particular kind of monster—that which is *unnamable*.

> "*A deplorable and most lamentable matter, full of bitterness and grief, a monstrous business. a thing that one cannot think of without affright, cannot hear without horror, transgressions unheard of, enormities and atrocities contrary to every sentiment of humanity...have reached our ears.*"

> — from King Philip IV of France's 1307 indictment of the Knights Templars

Monsters are figures charged with meaning—something more than merely nonhuman—signaling their foreign status with too many organs or not enough; or in the wrong place; a deviation from the corporeal order. Monsters are charged with horror and confusion

---

[1] In *Hine's Varieties: Chaos & Beyond*, Original Falcon Press, 2019.

because they threaten to destabilize all orders, upset all hierarchies; interruptions from those spaces which remain outside the law, evidence of promiscuous couplings. The Latin *monstrum* (from *monere*, a warning, a threat); a terrible prodigy, a sign of impending calamity; a messenger from another world, one that demanded interpretation. Monsters are profoundly ambiguous, showing the excesses, potentialities and variable configurations of flesh and form available, even whilst they are made abject and unnatural. Monsters show the limit of the human, and in doing so, call the very project of 'humanity' into question. Monsters collapse distinctions such as science vs. myth, the actual with the fictive, delirium and the 'real.' As Foucault says, "There is monstrosity only when the confusion comes up against, overturns, or disturbs civil canon, or religious law." Similarly, Kristeva's concept of the abject points to the necessity of the monstrous form—that which is expelled to maintain acceptable forms of subjectivity, yet can never fully be set apart. As she explains, it "draws me toward the place where meaning collapses."

Eliphas Levi's representation of Baphomet turned the amorphous into form—collapsed the unnamable and the unknowable into a static image, often theorized as elements held in opposition, the thermodynamic equilibrium beloved by the conservative injunction to establish balance rather, to seek excesses.

What magics might a Pansy Baphomet unfold? Something perverse, to be sure. Popular definitions of the perverse tend to coalesce around obsession, deviation, departure from the normative, straying off the path; sexualities which are non-productive. Originally a theological category, it gained its sexual dimension at the close of the nineteenth century, in sexology's ordering of inchoate desire through the grimoires of Kraft-Ebbing and Hirschfeld, in the creation of the subject through the disciplinary regimes of power. Desire became subjected to taxonomy, dissection, law, regulation; perverse acts became the truths of particular kinds of beings—perverts. But perversion is not a mode of being against which the majoritarian normal reifies itself. Perversion is a withdrawal from the compulsory and the regulative, a means of unbounding desire from linear trajectories.

Not a god, not a deity, this Baphomet has no dominion, no utility; is sufficient to itself, unproductive of anything. Baphomet as constant unfolding-event, a presence felt when skins writhe and unravel, in the enfolding and blurring of bodies, in the simultaneity of sound—hearing the cry of gulls together with the rumble of a passing train; drinking cold water from a warm plastic cup.

7

Are There 'Queer Pagan Mysteries'?

Not long after my essay on *Queering Deity* I received an email inviting me to participate in a 'Queer Pagan Mysteries' workshop (that's 'participate' with a price tag, of course). My answer was that I wasn't sure what constituted 'Queer Pagan Mysteries,' but that I'd be interested in finding out what was being referred to here.

The response to my diffidence was along the lines of that just as there are 'women's mysteries' that are common to all women, and 'men's mysteries' which all men share in, then why shouldn't we have 'Queer Mysteries' which all queer-identified people participate in, too? The workshop would be focused on 'sharing stories' to overcome difference and celebrate queer spirituality together. There'd be drumming, too (naturally); guided journeying (uh-huh); an invitation to connect with our queer ancestors in 'traditional societies,' and the final kicker was that this workshop wasn't being widely and publicly advertised, but was being sent to people the organisers felt 'resonated' with 'queer' energy.

"Okay," I replied, "do you mind if I forward your email to my friend, Lou? She's been involved in Queer Pagan Camp since its beginning. She runs Camden LBGT forum. She's a great drummer, here's a link to one of her articles"...and more in that vein. The reply was not wholly unexpected, that whilst the organisers were looking forwards at some point in the future to opening the workshops to queer women, this present workshop was for queer-identified men only. At which point, I politely declined the invitation, reflecting (not for the first time) that this was an example of incommensurability between various conceptions of the meaning of 'queer'.

My problems with the kind of approach to 'Queer Pagan Mysteries' outlined above are twofold. Firstly, it seems to be rooted in a kind of essentialism—the notion that 'all queer persons,' regardless of gender, race, culture, class, etc.—share similar experiences. This kind of essentialist discourse is, of course, familiar from second-wave feminism and the mythopoetic men's movement. But is this necessarily something queer-identified pagans want to reproduce uncritically? Queer Paganism, for me, entails a politics which rests on the recognition and celebration of difference rather than a call to discover an (essentialised) sameness. The acknowledgement of the plurality and multiplicity; the undoing of monopolies that is foundational to the act of 'queering religion.'

My other thought (which is related to the first) is that what constitutes 'Queer Pagan Mysteries'—or at least the parameters within which any such notion could emerge—have been set in advance, rather than emerging out of shared dialogue.

This exchange was productive, however, in that it started me reflecting on 'mysteries' in general, and what might constitute 'Queer Pagan Mysteries' in particular. 'Mysteries' is one of those terms that gets thrown around a lot, and has a wide range of meanings and inferences attached to it. Of course, attempting to unpack the notion of 'Mysteries' of itself invites the paradox; that mysteries are, almost by definition (at least the ones I looked at), unknowable, secret, closed off from non-participants. The very term 'mystery' comes from the

Greek *myein* meaning 'to close.' And we still don't know what the 'more' of the Eleusinian Mysteries was, although historians have pieced together much of the surrounding context. Sarah Iles Johnston, in her book, *Ancient Religions* (2007), lists five key criteria shared by many mystery cults in antiquity:

- Mystery cults demanded secrecy; initiates were forbidden to divulge what they had experienced.
- Mystery cults promised to improve initiates' situations in the present life and/or after death.
- Initiates garnered these advantages by establishing a special relationship with divinities during initiation.
- Mystery cults were optional supplements to civic religion, rather than competing alternatives.
- Myths were associated with the cults, which narrated tales of the cults' divinities.

In her discussion of how to interpret the mystery cults, Johnston points out that whilst the mysteries appear to share some features with rites of passage (and she notes that most parts of Greece, including Athens, home of the Eleusinian mysteries, had no formal rites of passage which explicitly changed adolescents into adults), and that the promise to give initiates access to valuable secrets bears some similarity to guild or professional initiations, what is striking about the mysteries is that they were not mutually exclusive. "One could be initiated into as many mystery cults as one desired and could afford; during the imperial period, wealthy individuals made a 'grand tour' of them." This she says, distinguishes them from rites of passage (such as the transition from adolescent to child), or membership of guilds. She also says that although there is some evidence of communal feasting or celebrations held between initiates (such as the *thiasos* of

Dionysiac initiates), that there is a lack of evidence that initiates of the mysteries felt an obligation to one another—that the bond between initiates was not based on codependence, but that of shared privilege, and that mystery initiations focused primarily on individuals—in initiations at Eleusis, for example, each initiate had his or her own *mystagogos.*

I think, if we're going to approach the possibility that there might be 'Queer Pagan Mysteries,' then it might be useful to examine the very notion of mysteries and how that might operate within a queer-pagan space. Does, for example, mysteries discourse work to bring participants together? If so, how does it work in terms of excluding others?

I frequently find that there's a tension between (a) the notion that mysteries are something which can only be understood through direct, personal experience, and (b) the necessity for having 'guardians' (i.e., teachers) who selectively provide cues and guidance to the deserving—those who have 'earned' a right. (Or at the very least, for workshop leaders providing a 'service' for others.) It might be useful to think of 'mysteries' (without the definitive article) in terms of creating/maintaining boundaries, and to what extent those boundaries require 'policing.'

In a previous essay I drew attention to the idea of viewing queer as an ethical process of engagement rather than an identity-formation, drawing on the work of Gavin Brown. In a recent article Gavin reiterates the idea that queer is an ethical process: "a process of trying to put into practice a set of ethical modes of engagement with sexual and gender difference rather than a simple identity category."[1] He points out that a key element of queer ethics is a commitment to an

---

[1] Brown, Gavin. 2011, p143.

autonomous process which is rooted in reciprocal and mutually beneficial relations with other participants. Autonomy is a relational process—always incomplete—and "can be found anywhere where people attempt to take control of their own lives and create what they desire for themselves rather than relying on others to deliver it for them"; and, "Autonomy is not an object that can be possessed, only a process that can be worked towards in conjunction with others." Autonomous modes of organising (in a variety of queer spaces—from activist groups such as Queeruption to spiritual spaces such as the Radical Faeries and Queer Pagan Camp) tend to favour a participatory, DIY ethos over passive consumption.

If we think of queer as an ethical relation, then what mysteries might we unfold together, out of a shared commitment to openness? And not only to sexual/gendered difference either, but to the widest possible multiplicities of affect. It seems to me that there are 'mysteries' borne out of mutual care and compassion—in a commitment to relating to others (bodied and unbodied) in ways that enable us to share both the exuberance of coming together and respecting difference at the same time.

If you would like a real 'queer pagan mystery' then I can only offer an example from the UK's Queer Pagan Camp. Why would three queer men rise at dawn, and in driving rain and furious gales, endure the elements to make blueberry pancakes for their friends?

The answer is simple. They promised they would.

8
Biography of a Kiss

Quite by accident, I ran into someone I'd not seen for over a quarter of a century. After the meeting, I went home, and out this popped. I cried buckets after I'd finished it. This short essay also appears in my 2019 book, *Hine's Varieties: Chaos & Beyond* (The Original Falcon Press).

When you kissed me, my world turned around.

1986. I'd come down for a coven meeting, but I don't remember the ritual. I just remember the kiss. You walked me to the station, but I don't recall the conversation. I just remember the kiss. As I boarded the train, you reached up, threw your arms about me, and kissed me. No gentle peck on the cheek, it was full-on lips to lips. That kiss turned my world around.

You took your time, as though it was the most natural, the most normal thing in the world. As though the other people on the platform, on the train, weren't there. Or didn't matter. And whilst the station was not exactly heaving with commuters, it was not empty either.

It was a scene familiar from a thousand movies and tv shows; the parting of lovers. A script I never thought I could participate in, at least not with another man. We were not lovers really, but that first public kiss, in the warmth and heat of a summer's day, turned my world around.

I sat on the train. It pulled out of the station. There was a guy sitting opposite me, his eyes wide as saucers like he couldn't believe what he'd just witnessed. The whole journey back he kept glancing at me, and I rejoiced in his shock. And the funny thing was, as it turned out, this guy was at the same college I was attending in York—albeit in a different department—and for the next few weeks, I kept catching him staring at me in horrified, or perhaps jealous, fascination.

I'd grown up kissing other boys. In school, playing at "Stingray" I usually got to play the part of Aqua Marina, the silent mermaid, which gave plenty of room for kissing. It seemed natural, until one day it wasn't, and the kissing stopped and the name-calling began. I came out to my parents at age 21, to have the whole thing wrapped in a blanket of frozen silence. I'd shared furtive fumblings in the darkness of clubs and alleyways; explored the fringes of polymorphous pleasures, but was still not confident or comfortable with my self and my desires as they always seemed to escape or confound any attempt at being this or being that kind of person. I certainly wasn't 'out' to most of my friends, although I suspect some of them were more aware than I supposed. Most of my friends were occultists of one kind or another, and I was just beginning to get angry about the sweeping generalizations that were everywhere at that time—the "we don't want any kinks in our circle ho ho ho" kind of comments, or the flat declarations that anyone who was gay, lesbian or bisexual "couldn't be involved in magic." I knew there was a gay world separate to the occult; I just didn't feel ready to be part of it. I hid and sought consolation in esoteric obsessions and fantasies of power.

But I remember the kiss. And that chance meeting, after 25 years of distance, brought it back. So, I just wanted to acknowledge that. Because when you kissed me that morning, my world turned around.

9

Bona Shamans

*R*ound *the Horne* was a British weekly radio comedy programme which aired between 1965 and 1968 on Sunday
afternoons, starring Kenneth Horne and a supporting cast.
It quickly became one of the most popular shows of the time, attracting a regular audience of 15 million listeners. It was structured as a
revue, and made heavy use of parody and satire. Two of its most
popular characters were Julian and Sandy, two outrageously camp,
out-of-work actors played by Hugh Paddick and Kenneth Williams.
Kenneth Horne would encounter Julian and Sandy in a variety of
settings, often through slightly risqué magazines which he claimed to
have purchased innocently. Julian and Sand's many (dubious) enterprises included "Rentachap" (domestic help), "Bona Drag" (a clothes
boutique), and "Bona Law", in which Julian famously proclaimed
"We've got a criminal practice that takes up most of our time"—a
double-entendre alluding to their homosexuality.

The sketches would invariably begin with Kenneth Horne saying
"Hello, is anyone there?" to which the reply would be "Ooh hello!
I'm Julian and this is my friend Sandy!" These sketches would involve
a liberal use of Polari, the gay slang code, of which Kenneth Horne
would either pretend ignorance, or attempt to use himself, much to
the delight of Julian and Sand. Listeners at home might understand
that the Polari phrases indicated that something rude or sexual was
being alluded to, but only gay listeners would fully get the jokes. If

Julian commented that "trade's been a bit rough lately," casual listeners might not understand that this could be a reference to 'rough trade'—a male partner who became violent after sex. In this way, *Round the Horne* was able to escape the notice of the censors and portray two openly homosexual men living happy and exuberant lives.

Round the *Horne* has remained popular ever since; the episodes are continually rebroadcast, and are available in a wide variety of formats.

But, what exactly is Polari? Polari is a form of gay slang or argot. It is particularly associated with the British underground gay scene of the 1950s, a period where homosexuals faced not only violence from other people, but public exposure and humiliation (the newspapers routinely published the names and addresses of men and women charged with homosexual activity). Those charged with homosexual offences received prison sentences, and were routinely subjected to aversion therapy using drugs, electro-shock and hormone injections. A common police tactic was to persuade anyone arrested that their sentence would be reduced if they implicated others. The police would frequently visit people at their place of work, compounding the public humiliation of exposure and arrest. Polari became a code language whereby homosexuals could speak to each other about their concerns and desires. It had different variants and permutations; theatrical Polari would have different terms than the Polari spoken by gay merchant-seamen or sailors. Polari evolved out of various sources, such as thieves' cant, East End rhyming slang, and the slang of dockers and sailors. A major source is thought to be parlyaree—the slang used by fairground and circus people as well as beggars, sex-workers and other marginal groups in the nineteenth century. According to Paul Baker, parlyaree found its way into London's theatreland and was picked up by gay actors and other theatre folk, and from there spread into the wider gay community.

I first encountered Polari when I worked for Psychic Press in the early 1990s, working in an office with James Thorpe, an older gay man. He also introduced me to the *Round the Horne* programmes, and I've been a fan ever since. *Bona Shamans*, which owes much to the original episode, *Bona Séances* (series 3, episode 13), is my tribute to them.

For more about Polari, check out Paul Baker's *Fantabulosa: A Dictionary of Polari and Gay Slang* (London, New York. Continuum, 2002)

§§§

With apologies to the shades of Kenneth Horne, Kenneth Williams, and Hugh Paddick.

I've been doing Pagan workshops for some time now, but recently attendance has dropped off. It's as though Pagans aren't interested in finding out about the role of the semicolon in the 300 laws of witchcraft anymore. So I thought I'd catch the current wave, and reinvent myself as a Shaman. Picking up a copy of "Mystic Muscles"—I buy it for the gardening section—I saw, between notices for Aura Massages and Tantric Hand Shandy Therapy, a small advert for Bona Shamans of Islington. So I thought I'd pop along and see what they could do for me.

"Hello is anybody there?"

"Hello I'm Julian and this is my friend Sandy."

"Oh hallo Mr. Hine. How lovely to varda your dolly old eek again. What can we do you for?"

"Well I'm interested in shamanism. What have you got?"

"We've got it all. From the top to the bottom of the sacred tree. Jules and me are trollers between the worlds, aren't we Jules? Cruising the length and breadth of infinity in search of the inner mysteries. In and out of the latties of the gods we are."

"Well, what does this do?" [picks up tubular object]

"That's a didg. A didg. A didgeridoo. And that's yer actual Aborigine that is."

"Well what 'doo' you do with it?"

"You blow it silly. Go on Jules. Show him how you blow it. No one blows like Jules, Mr. Hine. He's famous for it. They come from miles around to see Jules blow, don't they Jules? Famous for his technique, he is. Go on Jules, give it a good blow. Go on wrap your lips around it. Get a good grip on it."

"And what happens after you blow it?"

"We-ell, you become occupied by mystic forces. Jules is always getting occupied, aren't you Jules?"

"Yes. Frequently."

"Well perhaps not. But what kind of shamans are there?"

"Well there's your Celtic Shaman. Very butch they are. All bulging lallies and blonde riah. I can see a few problems there. [looks critically at Hine]

"There's yer New Age Dolly Mixture...

"Wait I've got it! The Horny god priest. Very popular yer horny god priest. Vada the scene. You sitting majestically, surrounded by dolly palones all hanging on your every word as you beat the sacred drum and toss the mystic rattle and call upon the Queen of the Faeries. Oh yes, very popular with faeries everywhere, yer basic horny priest. They come flocking as soon as they see one, don't they Jules. Yes. Flocking. You have beat them off...Faeries."

"Maybe I'll give that a go."

"Oooo innee bold Jules?" "Yes. Very bold. Very."

"Well you sit over there and shake your rattle and Jules will be the Queen of the faeries."

"What? I find that difficult to visualize..."

"Well it might be difficult for you ducky, but it'll be easy for Jules. O yes. Go on, just think of Jules all diaphanous and floating."

"OOoooOOOooo...OOoooOOOooo...OOoooOOOooo."

"Ooh there 'e goes Mr. Hine. He's being occupied by yer actual mystic forces."

"OOOoooOOO...oooOOaah...aaAAAh..."

"What's happening?"

"I am Titania the fairy queen
Don't be so bold, I may just scream,
In these wild woods we'll mince and play
We'll trade and troll until the break of day
In bijou bowers we'll palare gay
and wallop zhooshy 'til lilly chases us away."

"OOOoooOOO...oooOOaah...aaAAAh... ...aaAAAh...Ahh"

[long pause]

"Ooh I've come over all strange."

"Don't worry Jules, you were possessed. Ridden you were. By Titania. The great Dona Dolly herself."

"Yes. Titania."

"Well this all seems very fine. Could I book Titania—er—Jules for my Samhain workshop?"

"OOh no we can't possibly do that!"

"Whyever not?"

Well, I'm washing my riah that night."

fin.

A quick guide to the Polari used in 'Bona Shamans'

Bijou   Small, usually with a positive connotation. So, Bijou Bower—a cosy little hideaway in the woods, or perhaps a cottage.

Bold   A secondary meaning of bold in the *Oxford English Dictionary* is a shameless or audacious person. In the speech of *Round the Horne,* bold indicates a reference to, or a preference for homosexuality. To be bold is to be both outrageous and, therefore, gay.

Bona   Adjective: Good. Adverb: Well.

Dolly   A smart or attractive woman, or sometimes a man.

Dona   A woman.

Eek   The face.

Lallies   Legs.

Lattie   A house or a flat.

Lily   Lily Law. The police.

Mince   To walk in an affected manner.

Palare   To talk.

Palone   A woman or an effeminate male.

Riah   Hair. An example of the back-slang terms frequently used in Polari.

"That's your actual" A phrase often used by Julian and Sandy, as in "That's your actual French," prior to uttering a bit of mangled French—used to imply cultural sophistication.

Titivate To make oneself smart or pretty.

Trade   Noun. Sex between men, particularly in a casual sense. Sometimes a non-gay pickup, or a male sex-

worker. Sometimes used to denote gay men or
male sex workers as a group, or their collective
activity.

Troll   To walk around, particularly with the aim of picking up a bit of trade.

Varda   To look or to espy.

Wallop To dance.

Zhooshy Noun. Clothing. Also refers to ornamentation.
Verb. As in to comb one's riah. Or to go away, or
swallow something. Or to titivate oneself up.

10

Pan: The Vengeance of the Wild in "The Music on the Hill"

Throughout the Pan-themed literature of the early twentieth century, there runs a common theme: that the lure of Pan promises a return to a rural idyll—a nostalgia for both wild landscape and reunion with natural life; a distinctly antimodern turning away from the industrialized world, and the restrictions and regulations of polite society. Pan both guards and beckons into this wild terrain, opening up vistas of possibility beyond the ordered world of civilization. Yet the encounter with Pan can be terrible too; the call to encounter the wild is profoundly disturbing, and the unwary trespasser into Pan's domain may get more than they have bargained for.

In this essay I examine the presence of this savage, vengeful aspect of Pan in Saki's[1] 1911 short story, "The Music on the Hill".

The protagonist of "The Music on the Hill" is one Sylvia Seltoun, an archetypal, middle-class woman who, having recently married—despite hostility from the family and her husband's "unaffected indifference to women," has moved to the countryside with Mortimer, her spouse. Sylvia has, Saki informs us, a "School-of-Art," appreciation of landscape, and despite her name, has little more experience of nature than "leafy Kensington." She is singularly unprepared then, for an encounter with Pan, and begins to sense, as she explores her new

---

[1] a.k.a. H.H. Munro

dwelling, that there is a "wild open savagery...a stealthy linking of the joy of life with the terror of unseen things." Sylvia's rose-tinted view of the natural world leaves her completely unprepared for the unmanaged ferality of the countryside.

Her husband, Mortimer, startles her with his professed belief in Pan:

> *"'The worship of Pan never has died out,' said Mortimer.*
> *'Other newer gods have drawn aside his votaries from time to time, but he is the Nature-God to whom all must come back at last. He has been called the Father of all the Gods, but most of his children have been stillborn.'"*

Sylvia is somewhat dismissive of her husband's musings, but as her walks through the countryside continue, her uneasiness grows. Her first encounter with Pan is "a strange sound—the echo of a boy's laughter, golden and equivocal." Shortly after this, she stumbles upon a shrine to Pan in the woods: "A stone pedestal surmounted by a small bronze figure of a youthful Pan." She sees that a bunch of grapes has been left as an offering at the feet of the statue, and annoyed by this wastefulness, snatches the bunch from the pedestal. Then comes the direct encounter:

> *"Contemptuous annoyance dominated her thoughts as she strolled slowly homeward, and then gave way to a sharp feeling of something that was very near fright; across a thick tangle of undergrowth a boy's face was scowling at her, brown and beautiful, with unutterably evil eyes. It was a lonely pathway, all pathways round Yessney were lonely for the matter of that, and she sped forward without waiting to give a closer scrutiny to this sudden apparition. It was not till she*

had reached the house that she discovered that she had dropped the bunch of grapes in her flight."

Later, in describing this uncanny encounter to her husband, Sylvia supposes that the youth might have been a "gypsy lad." He warns her that her meddling might well have unpleasant consequences:

> *"'I don't think you were wise to do that," he said reflectively. 'I've heard it said that the Wood Gods are rather horrible to those who molest them.'*
>
> *'Horrible perhaps to those that believe in them, but you see I don't,' retorted Sylvia.*
>
> *'All the same,' said Mortimer in his even, dispassionate tone, 'I should avoid the woods and orchards if I were you, and give a wide berth to the horned beasts on the farm.'"*

On her subsequent walk though, despite her dismissal of her husband's fanciful warning, Sylvia hears a "low, fitful piping, as of some reedy flute" from a nearby copse, and in her imagination links it to the restlessness of a usually docile ram. Continuing her walk, she hears the baying of hunting hounds in chase, and espies a large stag. She fears that the stag will be brought down by the dogs right in front of her, but at the last moment, the pipe music she heard before thrills about her, and the stag bears down upon her. At the last, she sees that she is not alone:

> *"'Drive it off!' she shrieked. But the figure made no answering movement.*
>
> *The antlers drove straight at her breast, the acrid smell of the hunted animal was in her nostrils, but her eyes were filled with the horror of something she saw other than her oncoming*

death. And in her ears rang the echo of a boy's laughter,
golden and equivocal."

With that shocking moment, the story ends, Sylvia gored by the
stag, but her eyes "filled with the horror of something she saw other
than her oncoming death"—perhaps a vision of Pan?

Central to *The Music on the Hill* is the theme of transgression. Not
only does Sylvia transgress against the presence of Pan in her removal
of the offered bunch of grapes, but her very marriage to Mortimer,
her prying him away from his town life, and her abortive attempt to
settle him down in his country house can be seen as transgressions
against a male homosociality she is scarcely aware of: a hidden life in
the countryside, and perhaps, one in London, too. Saki tells us that,
"She had watched with satisfaction the gradual fading of what she
called 'the Jermyn-Street-look' in his eyes as the woods and heather of
Yessney had closed in on them." Jermyn Street, named after its
founder, Henry Jermyn was a mixture of residential dwellings, hotels,
theatres, gentleman's clubs, tea-rooms and shops, but it was also a
notorious queer haunt. In the eighteenth century, Jermyn Street was
the site of a brothel-house that catered for men who enjoyed the company of 'mollies,' and in the nineteenth-century, the street hosted a
male-only Turkish bath. It is notable that another of Munro's short
stories, *The Recessional*, takes place in the Jermyn Street Turkish Bath.

Also home to some of Britain's most-well known tailors, the
'Jermyn-Street-look' indicates a degree of raffishness, even dandyism.
(There's a bronze statue of tastemaker George Bryan 'Beau' Brummel
in Jermyn Street.) It might also be read as indicating an intensely
homosocial sensibility—by 1895, there were no fewer than thirty

gentlemen's clubs around St. James.[2] Roy Porter (1994) points out that, "Clubs helped keep London a masculine city, and St James's, with its bachelor chambers around King and Jermyn Streets, was its inner sanctum."

> *"'You will never get Mortimer to go,' his mother had said carpingly, 'but if he once goes he'll stay; Yessney throws almost as much a spell over him as Town does. One can understand what holds him to Town, but Yessney—' and the dowager had shrugged her shoulders."*

If Sylvia Seltoun is unaware of her husband's secret life in the city, she is equally unsuspecting of the threat to compulsory heteronormativity that lurks in the countryside of Yessney. Unable to see past her urban complacency and her vague religious sentiments, she is unprepared for her otherwise remote and distant husband's passionate avowal of the reality of Pan's presence, and his warning of the danger she has placed herself in by disturbing the shrine. It is whilst following the path taken by her husband on one of his mysterious peregrinations—"farm and woods and trout-streams seemed to swallow him up from dawn till dusk"—that she encounters the shrine to Pan. She guesses that Mortimer has placed the grapes by the statue of Pan as an offering, but dismisses it as "a harmless piece of lunacy." The bunch of grapes may point in the direction of Bacchus or Dionysus, but the hint is there that Mortimer is pursuing his own course—'honoring Pan'—as much separate from her as he was in his life in the town.

The pipe-playing youth, who is either avatar or presentiment of the onset of Pan, is a stock figure in the Pan-themed literature, appearing in a variety of forms and guises—for example, as Tommy Duffin

---

[2] See Milne-Smith, 2011, pp32–33.

in Dunsany's *The Blessing of Pan* and Eustace, in E.M. Forster's *The
Story of a Panic*. Usually, this figure is male, corresponding to the
Daphnis ephebe, but occasionally there are female Pan-children (for
example, Elspeth, in Algernon Blackwood's *A Touch of Pan*).
Sylvia describes this youth in ambivalent terms: "brown and beautiful, with unutterably evil eyes" and later, "brown-faced and rather
handsome, but a scoundrel to look at." She supposes, to her husband,
that he is a "gypsy lad." According to Abby Bardi, the appearance of
gypsies in British literature was frequently a dual signification—they
are a "symbol of escape from the dominant social mores governing sex
and gender roles and the ownership of capital," and at the same time,
are reviled as primitive and feared. In *The Music on the Hill*, it is
unclear whether or not this wild youth—described in a similar way to
the similarly feral *Gabriel-Ernest*—is a supernatural creature or a
human, although Mortimer Seltoun seems to hint that the youth is of
the order of the "Wood Gods." Again, this recalls Sandy Bryne's
observation that "The object of desire in Saki's stories is often adolescent and inhuman, or at least outside human society, and therefore
constraints of class, manners, and mores."[3]

---

[3] Bryne, 2007, p115.

Queerying Paganisms:
Bibliography

Baker, Paul. 2002. *Fantabulosa: A Dictionary of Polari and Gay Slang.* Continuum.

Bardi, Abbi. 'The Gypsy as Trope in Victorian and Modern British Literature.' *Romani Studies 5* Vol. 16, No.1 (2006), 31–42.

Blanshard, Alistair. 2010. *Sex: Vice and Love from Antiquity to Modernity.* Wiley-Blackwell.

Brown, Gavin. 2011. 'Amateurism and anarchism in the creation of autonomous queer spaces' in Heckert, Jamie; Cleminson, Richard (eds.). *Anarchism & Sexuality: Ethics, Relationships and Power.* Routledge.

Brown, Norman O. 1966. *Love's Body.* Random House.

Byrne, Sandi. 2007. *The Unbearable Saki: The Work of H.H. Munro.* Oxford University Press, reprint edn.

Cohen, Jeffrey J. 2003. *Medieval Identity Machines.* University of Minnesota Press.

Dinshaw, Carolyn. 1999. *Getting Medieval: Sexualities and Communities, Pre- and Postmodern.* Duke University Press.

Flood, Gavin. 2006. *The Tantric Body: The Secret Tradition of Hindu Religion.* I.B. Tauris.

Gaiman, Neil. 1991. *Sandman: The Dream Country.* DC Comics.

Grafton, Anthony; Most, Glenn W.; Settis, Salvatore. 2010. *The Classical Tradition.* Harvard University Press.

Harris, Adrian. 2013. 'Honouring the Outcaste Dead', *Fieldwork in Religion*, Vol 8, No 2 (2013), Equinox Publishing Ltd.

Harris, Judith. 2009. *Pompeii Awakened: A Story of Rediscovery.* I.B. Tauris.

Hausner, Sondra L. 2016. *The Spirits of Crossbones Graveyard: Time, Ritual, and Sexual Commerce in London.* Indiana University Press.

Hine, Phil. 2019. *Hine's Varieties: Chaos & Beyond.* Original Falcon Press.

Johnston, Sarah Iles. 2007. *Ancient Religions.* Harvard University Press.

Kaye, Richard A. 2008. 'Sexual identity at the fin de siècle' in Marshall, Gail (ed.), *The Cambridge Companion to the Fin de Siècle.* Cambridge University Press.

Kendrick, Walter. 1997. *The Secret Museum: Pornography in Modern Culture.* University of California Press.

Matthews, Caitlin & John. 2003. *Walkers Between the Worlds: The Western Mysteries from Shaman to Magus.* Inner Traditions.

Mattusch, Carol C. 2005. *The Villa dei Papiri at Herculaneum: Life and Afterlife of a Sculpture Collection.* Getty Publications.

Milne-Smith, Amy. 2011. *London Clubland: A Cultural History of Gender and Class in Late-Victorian Britain.* Palgrave MacMillan.

Mitter, Partha. 1977. *Much Maligned Monsters: A History of European Reactions to Indian Art.* University of Chicago Press.

Nardizzi, Vin; Guy-Bray, Stephen. (eds.). 2009. *Queer Renaissance Historiography: Backward Gaze.* Ashgate.

Norton, Rictor (ed.), "The Times by Charles Churchill, 1764", *Homosexuality in Eighteenth-Century England: A Sourcebook.* Updated 1 Dec. 1999. <http://rictornorton.co.uk/eighteen/1764chur.htm>.

Porter, Roy. 1994. *London: A Social History.* Penguin Books.

Serres, Michel. 1997. *Genesis.* University of Michigan Press.

Varone, Antonio. 2001. *Erotica pompeiana: love inscriptions on the walls of Pompeii.* L'Erma di Bretschneider.

Vicinus, Martha. 1999. "The Adolescent Boy: Fin-de-Siècle Femme Fatale?" in Dellamora, Richard (ed.), *Victorian Sexual Dissidence.* University of Chicago Press.

Wilde, Oscar. 1908, 1992. *The Picture of Dorian Gray.* Wordsworth Classics.

Two: *Queerying* Tantras

My interest in the Tantric traditions began with a recurring dream of Kali; she appeared nightly, outlined in flame; hair unbound; laughing wildly and seeming to leer suggestively as she gestured towards the flame of a funeral pyre. I had, by that point, heard of Kali, but I did not *know* her; I did not feel any draw or pull to her. She disturbed me, and that put the hook in me.

Years later, I encountered tantric teachers and eventually took various initiations. After practicing for about a decade, I began to realize something important. Whilst I had pursued various practices—ritual, meditation, mantras, etc.—I had largely done so without engaging with the philosophy/theology underpinning them, or the cultural context in which they are inextricably embedded. In other words, I was still understanding the tantras from my familiar background ('Western' occultism and other categories of knowledge). This is, in part, what led to my interest in examining histories; many of the misconceptions which remain in circulation regarding the nature of the tantras arose during the colonial period. I began to want to know more about the origin of these ideas, and why they still persist today. At the same time, I began a deep dive into the tangled history of the tantric traditions and the other religions of India. As I became more comfortable with identifying as queer, I began to look for 'evidence' of a queer sensibility in these traditions. What I discovered was wonderful. Indian religions have developed a dizzying array of concepts relating to gender and sexuality, but few of them can easily be assimilated into Euro-American modes of understanding.

They were, for me, an invitation to think differently. It is often challenging and difficult to take this kind of approach. I struggle at times. The texts are difficult to understand. The largely academic texts that discuss and elaborate on these traditions, even more so. It is worth it, for they open up new worlds and new encounters—new possibilities of relation to ourselves and our world.

The three essays I've chosen for this section question the easy assumptions often made about the Tantric traditions and contemporary 'Western' notions of sexual identity and difference, and how they impact on practice. I tend to view the queerness of the tantric traditions not in terms of particular desires, but in terms of how those traditions are excessive. It is the deep sense of jubilance that I find queer—the commitment to wonder, joy, indeterminacy and playfulness as the very foundation of life.

11

On Tantra and
Heteronormativity

"To fit perfectly a man needs a woman, a woman needs a man. They are polar opposites, and that polarity is needed. It is just as if you are trying to create electricity without polar opposites, without positive and negative."

— Osho

"If liberation could be attained simply by having intercourse with a śakti, then all living beings in the world would be liberated just by having intercourse with women."

— *Kularnavatantra*

I've been engaged in some thought-provoking correspondence of late. One person recently commented: "Don't you find that traditional tantra is well, really heteronormative?"

What is "Traditional Tantra"?

This in itself raises the question of what constitutes 'traditional' tantra. I often come across authors attempting to periodise tantra into 'historical' vs. 'modern'—where 'historical' is the texts and practises that came out of India (and Tibet, China, Japan, etc.), and 'modern' is what contemporary writers and practitioners are doing. But such distinctions are tricky. After all, tantra is a *living* tradition, and many of the texts, practises and ideas that I've raised on *enfolding* from time to time are still being used, discussed and reworked on a worldwide basis. Of course, 'tradition' is a door that swings both ways, as it were—it can be used to signify something which is more 'authentic' than the present; or equally, something that, compared to the contemporary, is antiquated and of not much relevance. How do you decide though, whether or not something is 'historical' in the first place? Take the *Kularnavatantra* ('ocean of the heart tantra'), for example. It is thought to have been written (or compiled) somewhere between the 10th and 14th centuries CE which, you might think, qualifies it to be 'historical.' But it is one of the most widely quoted and circulated tantric texts amongst contemporary tantra practitioners, regardless of sectarian affiliation.

As it turned out, for this particular correspondent, 'traditional tantra' meant the tantra-sacred-sex workshops and writings he'd encountered—which tend to be grounded (to varying degrees) in discourses of gender polarity and other binary oppositions. This brings me to another popular distinction which is often drawn, between 'Classical' and 'Neo-tantra.'

"Classical vs. Neo-Tantra"

Here, 'classical' tantra is often used to denote the 'original' tantra (which emerged from India and other parts of Asia), and 'Western' tantra (a.k.a. 'sacred sex'). The term 'Neo-tantra' was originally coined by Georg Feuerstein to make a distinction between what he saw as authentic tantra, and what he referred to as 'Californian Tantra' which, in his view, was "based on a profound misunderstanding of the Tantric path." Some contemporary exponents of neo-tantra argue, however, that Western approaches to tantra have removed the elitism (i.e., the precondition of initiation & transmission of knowledge via a guru), lengthy dependence on ritual (and its underlying theology), and the emphasis on worldly power which can be found in some classical tantras. How useful is this distinction? In his *Tantra Illuminated,* Christopher D. Wallis argues that the term 'Tantra' has come to be almost entirely detached from its original meanings, and that for the most part, the New Age and alt.spirituality teachers who deploy it have no connection to the original tradition. He points out that making a distinction between modern, neo- or 'Western' Tantra and 'original' or 'classical' Indian Tantra does not necessarily imply that the former is illegitimate, but what he does challenge are the claims to historicity that some modern teachers make. Wallis makes the valid point that if what is being taught is effective and helpful, then New Age teachers don't need, surely, to make a historical claim.[1] In some ways, as Hugh B. Urban points out in his *Tantra: Sex, Secrecy, Politics and Power in the Study of Religion,* "...the imagining of Tantra will be different in every historical moment and in every new cross-cultural encounter."[2] It's undeniable, I think, that 'tantra' now operates as a kind of generic, globalised brand-image that is so caught up with contemporary representations of sexuality— and in particular, sex therapy, healing and sexual liberation—that no amount of finger-wagging and distinction-making is going to dislodge it. Many people who encounter tantra in this context are surprised (at least judging from some of the comments I get) that there are other 'kinds' of tantra which are, at times, seemingly at odds with the tantra/ sacred-sex representation, and that these tantras are widely practiced by people all over the world.

---

[1] Wallis, 2012, p432.
[2] Urban, 2003, p272.

On heteronormativity

But leaving the problems of periodisation and sorting out classical vs. modern aside, let's come back to the heteronormativity issue. One of my correspondents wrote: "You must have noticed that a lot of people who do tantra training and workshops are very heterosexually-oriented and go on about male-female polarity." Well, yes. Apart from a few exponents of tantra who are questioning such tropes, these are fairly common themes in the tantra-as-sacred-sex workshop circuit. What interests me particularly though, is where these ideas came from. Do these ideas reflect attitudes found in pre-colonial cultures? And for that matter, is heteronormativity even a concept that we can apply to say, pre-colonial India or Japan? Did these cultures even have a notion of 'compulsory heterosexuality' in the same way that we've come to view contemporary European culture?

Heteronormativity, a term originally coined by Michael Warner, refers to the ways in which majoritarian society constructs and reifies the assumption that heterosexuality is made normal, inevitable and compulsory—and casts both non-heterosexual desiring subjects and some forms of heterosexuality—as marginal and deviant.

Heteronormativity is not simply about desiring subjects though—it encompasses a wide range of social practices and institutions, ranging from deeply-held cultural norms about the body, to class, race, the state, consumption and concepts of personal freedom.[3]

Heteronormativity isn't just a fancy way of referring to heterosexuality, nor, as Annamarie Jagose points out (2012) is it merely a consequence of the bifurcated categories of heterosexuality and homosexuality, but heteronormativity as a critical concept indexes

---

[3] Warner, 1991, xiii.

the emergence of heterosexuality as a function of the modern disciplinary regime of sexuality.

Heteronormativity can be thought of as a complex regime of disciplinary power which regulates sexual and social identities and practices—granting ideal, normative status and privilege to (some forms of) heterosexuality as the basis of social identity and excluding others.

Again, I'm going to leave the question of heteronormativity in relation to precolonial India aside (for now) as it's my contention that the gender essentialism that is so prevalent in much of contemporary approaches to tantra arises from sacred-sex discourse itself.

"Reverse Kundalini"?

When I first started to get interested in tantra in the early 1980s, binary gender essentialism was all too common in many popular books on tantra and 'sacred sex.' In fact, there were a lot of people stating fairly unequivocally that if you weren't heterosexual, you couldn't do tantra—for various reasons, all of which I came to view as spurious. A book I found particularly irritating, was Nik Douglas and Penny Slinger's best-selling *Sexual Secrets* (first published in 1979), which was hailed as "the definitive, all-encompassing text on sacred sexuality," and which made many statements about male homosexuality, although they didn't seem to mind too much about two women getting it on. They asserted that male homosexuals transmit karma, as well as hormones and vitality via anal or oral sex. Rather than campaign for 'acceptance,' such men should practice yoga for "overcoming the wiles of destiny."[4] The two authors confidently asserted that sex between men was totally unheard of in India until

---

[4] Douglas, Slinger, *Sexual Secrets,* 1979. In later editions, some of these views appear to have been toned down somewhat.

the Moslem invasions, and that sex between men was not 'traditional' in either China or Japan. They also stated that acceptance of male homosexuality was the cause of the downfall of the Greeks and the Roman Empire—something of a warning, no doubt, to the modern West.

I went through stages of being initially confused by these pronouncements, to being annoyed—and challenging these views through writing, public speaking (and occasionally just being a camp-ish presence at occult events)—to largely deciding to ignore them as far as my own practice went. Something I found particularly lacking in books on tantra at the time, was any reference to tantra as a *magical* practice. This was basically where my interests lay, rather than what seemed to be an ever-present emphasis on a Western biomedical model of sexuality, which presented sex as an innate drive contained within the body, untroubled by differences of culture or historicity.

It all seemed very factual, and much of it was presented as immu-table cosmic laws or psychological and 'scientific' theories (Freud and Jung being particularly popular), which were applied to everyone without exception. In this, sacred-sex advocates largely followed the pronouncements of turn-of-the-century sexologists (hardly surpris-ing given that sexologists and sex therapists have become the new 'tantric gurus'), and much colonial-era writing about India. Some seem to have uncritically taken the view that Indian civilisation was static and unchanging—and only had 'traditions'—whereas only the West was capable of progress and change. This kind of romanticism can quickly shade into racist ideas about sexuality and primitivism.

It wasn't until I started reading the work of Sir John Woodroffe (a.k.a. Arthur Avalon), and found some copies of the AMOOKOS[5] magazine *Azoth* that I began to make inroads into quite a different presentation of tantra—and largely left all the 'sacred sex' stuff behind. It seemed to me that what these 'sacred sex' books and their advocates were promoting was a kind of liberation—sexual libera-tion—that only applied to heterosexual couples and encouraged experimentation whilst at the same time setting boundaries for the 'normal,' and relegating anything they disapproved of into the cate-gory of 'the perverse' backed up with dodgy justifications about reverse kundalini, etc.

Gradually though, ideas changed, and the boundaries of what con-stituted 'sacred sex' began to accommodate (to varying degrees) non-heterosexuals. Ashley Thirleby's little book, *Tantra: The Key to Sexual Power and Pleasure* (1982), was one of the first books I came across which, although "written for heterosexual couples" at least allowed that "...the Rituals of the Seven Nights of the Tantra are equally intended for, and adaptable for, use by homosexual couples." By 1989, Margot Anand was making similar accommodative state-ments, noting that although her book was addressed to heterosexual partners, she knew that the practices it detailed were "beneficial to partners of the same sex." Anand, in a reversal of the Douglas & Slinger position, says that: "In the ancient Hindu and Greek tradi-tions of sacred sexuality, as well as in many other cultures, there were no such judgements about loving a person of the same gender." She was, at least in this edition of *The Art of Sexual Ecstasy,* unwilling to move away from the notion of gender polarity, arguing that for her

---

[5] AMOOKOS: The *Arcane and Mystical Order of the Knights of Shambala*—an East-West Tantric Order.

"High Sex"—the goal of the practice—was for individuals to explore "the masculine and feminine aspects of his or her nature," and that these polarities were present in everyone. She stated that in same-sex couples, it is likely that one partner will have dominant male qualities, whilst the other is more feminine.[6]

Barbara Carrellas' (2007) *Urban Tantra: Sacred Sex for the Twenty-First Century* takes the perspective that the 'myth' that tantra has to be done by a man and a woman has "kept more queer people out of tantra than any other myth." In posing the question of "How did this myth start?" Carellas states that "...Tantra, being the path of acceptance of everything, has always embraced opposites: good/evil, sacred/profane, higher/lower, earthly/spiritual, yin/yang, light/shadow."[7]

What's notable here is that although Carellas seems to accept that binary gender essentialism is a Western misunderstanding of tantra, she still treats her list as transcultural universals, rather than Western binarisms that may not even be applicable to tantra. Although she later says that "yin and yang can no longer be assigned according to the shape of one's genitals," she goes on to imply that yin and yang are related to hormones, and that individuals with a predominance of testosterone tend to be more yang, whilst those with oestrogen-dominant bodies tend to be more yin. Even whilst she states that gender is more of a "rainbow" than an either-or proposition, Carellas seems loath to totally move away from the gender binary.

Some closing thoughts

So, back to the original question: is tantra heteronormative? It depends. If you're talking about the way that tantra has emerged as

---

[6] Anand, 1989.
[7] Carellas, 2007, p9.

an element within the wider discourse of 'sacred sex,' then yes, you could make that case. As I said, it's my contention that this is a result of the ways that sexology, sex therapy, and other disciplinary regimes had made use of tantric themes, or at least creatively re-interpreted them to bolster up the inevitability and normalcy of heterosexuality. But this is now changing, as more queer-identified people are challenging these views and engaging directly with tantric texts.

If, however, you mean 'classical' tantra, then this is something worth looking into, but it might be a more difficult proposition.

12

Ardhanarishvara and Other Conundrums of Gender

If they see
breasts and long hair coming they call it woman,
if beard and whiskers they call it man:
But, look, the self that hovers in between
is neither man nor woman O Ramanatha.

— Dasimayya

I had an enquiry recently from someone who wanted me to help them compile a list of 'queer-friendly' Hindu deities—'queer-friendly' apparently meaning, 'deities who shift shape/gender.' My response highlighted some of the problems with approaching deities in this way:

Firstly, it'd probably be easier, with respect to India, to find gods or goddesses who *don't* shift shape or gender as being exceptional.

Secondly, the presence of shape/gender-shifting deities or myths does not necessarily equate with Indian culture having a 'positive attitude' towards queer-identified people—even in pre-colonial India. Two early mediaeval texts, Vatysana's *Kamasutra* (3rd–4th century CE) and Vararuci's *Ubhayabhisarika*—a satirical monologue play written between the 4th–6th century CE—both mention courtesans who are of the so-called 'third nature' *(trtiyaprakrti),* but a close reading of both texts reveals that the status of these courtesans is highly ambiguous.

Thirdly, if you're going to look at shape/gender-shifting in Indian culture, then I would stress that it's more useful to do so in terms of what those actions signify within Indian culture—and not just from a Western perspective. Although some degree of comparison is probably inescapable, I believe that it is useful to at least try to find out what those acts mean within the various Indian contexts in which they are situated. It's likely that there will be significant differences—some of which may take us to unexpected, and possibly uncomfortable places.

Ardhanarishvara—beyond gender?

Ardhanarishvara—*the Lord Who is Half Woman*—is often interpreted in quasi-Jungian terms; i.e., taken as 'symbolic' of the union of opposites, the bringing together of oppositional polarities, of wholeness and balance. This is a common way to interpret Ardhanarishvara —in terms of being 'symbolic' of these qualities—but I want to suggest that such symbolic representations can lead to other possibilities being overlooked.

I was flipping through the *Kularnava Tantra* one morning on the way to the office when I came across a *dhyana* (a scene for meditation) which begins,

> *"One should in his heart-lotus, first contemplate Ardhanarishvara Lord Śiva in the following manner: in the middle of the ocean of nectar embellished there is a raised island. On it in the woodland of Kalpa-trees there is a beautiful canopy of nine rubies. In that canopy there is a throne embellished with nine jewels. On that throne in the pericarp of the lotus, is seated Lord Śiva decorated with Moon and Sun*

and Devi Ambika forming half of his body. The ornaments of both are glittering on their bodies. Beautiful as tens of millions of Kama devas and always young as a sixteen-year-old, the lotus face of Lord Ardhanarishvara mildly smiles. He has three eyes and the Moon decorates his hair.... Accompanied by Vidya and Siddhis He is always blissful. Innumerable gods mentioned in Mahāsodhā are waiting in his service. One should contemplate upon such a form of Ardhanarishvara Lord Śiva, in the heart-lotus."

The verse that follows though, is what I want to focus attention on:

"One can contemplate upon Ardhanarishvara either in a Masculine or in a Feminine form, or in saccindanada— Attributeless form which is full of all radiance and contains all the mobile and immobile creation."

Now this, I'd say, illustrates some of the complexities of approaching Indian ideas of gender in respect to deities (of which there are many). Firstly, we have Ardhanarishvara (i.e., Śiva-Śakti). Then we have the verse saying that we can think of deity as male or female, but that *superior* to these is the 'attributeless' form: *saccindanda* (a compound term sometimes translated as 'being-consciousness-bliss').

A word or two about Śiva-Śakti. The Śiva-Śakti pairing which is a striking feature of many Indian traditions—particularly 'tantric' traditions—is all too often interpreted within the framework of European notions of binary dualities or polarities—and from there, into (for example) Jung's concept of the *coniunctio oppositorum*—the 'conjunction of opposites.' However, these representations (which are very popular) tend to ignore the way that Śiva-Śakti is described in textual sources. Śiva-Śakti are inseparable from each other in the way that the heat and light of a flame are inseparable. Some texts tend to prioritise Śiva in relation to Śakti, whilst others hold Śakti as 'superior' to Śiva; others give them 'equal' status; in fact, it is not unusual to find all three positions expressed within a single text. On a cautionary note, however, it is too simplistic to seek a one-to-one correspondence between these 'theological' concepts of 'divine gender' and social reality—or even the way that Śiva and Śakti are used to support the ubiquitous lists of male and female 'principles' which seem to be common to so many popular representations of tantra. (It may be useful for queer practitioners to reflect on how 'polarity'—as a categorising activity—acts to support heteronormativity.)

In the earlier essay on the issue of *Queering Deity*, I commented that: "We are used, in Western culture, to thinking of ourselves as bounded, stable individuals possessing a fixed essence, (a particular sexuality, for example) agency and limitations, that we tend to represent deities in the same way." So, we tend to think of shifts in shape/gender as being particular to certain deities and not others, rather than a general capacity.

In nondual tantric (and other Hindu) theologies, the gods are 'beyond' gender in a sense. Gender only comes into operation at the level of 'Maya.' I'll try to keep this brief. Cosmic evolution is a progressive unfolding of the formless and unknowable into myriad diverse forms—the goddess playing hide and seek with herself, is how I like to think of it sometimes—via the operation of various 'powers' which are themselves extensions of the actions of Śiva (or Lalita). Maya, which is often interpreted as 'illusion' but can equally be thought of as 'enchantment' or 'playfulness'—is a process of making distinctions and discriminations into myriad forms to the extent that they become limited beings who have 'forgotten' their divine origin. That we may understand this, Lalita (for instance) takes on myriad forms as part of her playfulness (one of the meanings of Lalita is 'playful').

Tantric texts sometimes state that deity has three aspects: form, subtle and very subtle. Form—which is basically the iconographic 'image' of the deity in human form—isn't so much an 'individual subject, possessing particular characteristics' (although that's how we interact with them), but a 'gateway' which can lead us towards the all-encompassing presence of the deity. The 'subtle' represents the deity-as-mantra (which is to say, deities are mantras and *vice versa),* and the 'very subtle' form is deity-as-yantra[1]. In some texts, the subtler aspects are said to be superior to the 'form' aspect. You start out relating to Lalita as a deity-form, and then progress to Lalita-as-mantra, and then to Lalita-as-yantra. I prefer to say that all 3 aspects are interrelated; my own practice utilises all three simultaneously.

The upshot of all of this is that if you want to relate to any deity as male, female, trans-gendered or ungendered, formed or formless (or any combination thereof) then that's okay if that's what you need to do. What's more important is that you relate to deity in the first place; that you do the practice (and gradually, you might come to the reali-sation that deity 'encompasses' all these forms—and that all these forms are, ultimately, deity). This is the nondual approach.

The perspective that deity can be multiply-gendered is not restricted to Ardhanarishvara. Nammalvar, a 9th century CE Tamil poet, who in his poems expressed his devotion to Vishnu in the voice of a young woman in love (or that of her mother, or a concerned

---

[1] A yantra, in this instance, is a deity represented in a geometrical array. The supreme deity is at the centre, with attendants or subsidiary deities arrayed around them in tiers or circles. A yantra can represent the unfolding sequence of the central deities' activities in the world.

female friend), wrote of Vishnu in these multiple gender registers—
as both mother, father, and encompassing all genders:

> *"Neither male nor female, nor is he neuter.*
> *He cannot be seen, he's not one who is,*
> *nor one who's not.*
> *When you desire him, he takes the form*
> *of your desire,*
> *but he's not that either:*
> *it's very hard indeed to speak about my Lord."*

In her essay, *Gender in a Devotional Universe* (2003), Vasudha
Narayanan examines the religious practises of the SriVaishnava community, including a yearly ritual that takes place at some Vaishnava
temples, attracting thousands of devotees: an image of Nammalvar is
dressed as a beautiful woman, and taken to meet 'her' lover, Vishnu,
an event celebrated in both song and ritual.

Some Problems

The lure of the symbolic

The problem of 'symbolic thinking' (useful though it is) is twofold. Firstly, symbols are often interpreted in a globalised, universal
manner—which is to say that one might take Western concepts of
'androgyny' and interpret Ardhanarishvara entirely within that
framework—and not consider other (i.e., different South Asian)
interpretations. Secondly, there is a problem with symbolic thinking
itself. Thinking of images and forms entirely as being 'symbolic of
something' requires a kind of deferral—a gap—between object and
its meaning, between signifier and signified. This can result in a kind
of refusal to 'see' an object as it is—and get lost in a seemingly endless
maze of symbols—none of which may have any direct relevance to

the object being attended to. I'll try to illustrate how some Indian theologies offer a different perspective via the medium of *Darśana*. *Darśana* can be thought of as a primary mode of communication between deity and devotee. So, to 'see' Ardhanarishvara, or to receive Ardhanarishvara's *Darśana* simultaneously, is to see the deity but also to be *seen* by the deity. It is both a recognition of the deity's 'presence' in the world, but also arouses and stirs the appropriate passion which kindles the relationship between devotee and deity. In looking at a visual image, in visualising Ardhanarishvara's image as dwelling in the heart, in the recitation of *stotra* and mantra, one is not dealing with symbols, but with actualities. To visualise Ardhanarishvara dwelling in one's heart is to feel—i.e., viscerally experience—the embodied presence of deity.

The lure of lists

I sometimes feel that in the rush to find resonances with contemporary Euro-American instance of 'queer' with other cultures, and back into premodern history, it's too easy to find similarities, but ignore differences. P. Sufinas Virius Lupus, in a blog post in 2012, expresses this problem very well:

> *"...when we look at things from the past or from other cultures, we tend to go 'Oh, a non-binary gender identity = queer,' or 'a male having sex with a male = queer,' or anything else ad infinitum.*
>
> *And, unfortunately, that often ignores that what is going on in those societies—though perhaps not typical—is often completely acceptable."*[2]

---

[2] http://aediculaantinoi.wordpress.com/2012/05/03/when-queer-isnt-or-what-are-the-boundaries-of-queer/

Although list-making can be useful, there is a kind of politics in list-making as practice. It's interesting to see who or what gets to appear on lists, and who or what is omitted—and often the criteria for including, for example, one gender-swapping deity whilst excluding another, isn't made explicit. Lists decontextualise 'objects' from their surroundings, and recontextualise them with reference to other items listed—and all too often, this is done from the perspective of a top-down 'grand theory'—Jungian archetypes, for example—which takes a range of examples from different contexts and effectively collapses them into aspects of each other. These collapses can quickly become reifications—'evidence' of the global ubiquity of a particular trend or category of organisation. Lawrence Cohen, for example, is critical of scholarly moves which tend to position the notion of 'third gender' into a global category:

> *"Academics are persons of various genders who sometimes utilise conceptions of third gender as metaphors in social theory. But though third gender is good to think with, its theorization is often exquisitely insensitive to the bodies with which it plays"*[3]

And in particular the way that category of 'third gender'

> *"invokes a global semantic network (encompassing caricatures of transsexual, berdache, xanith, hijra, mah'u, androgynous, hermaphroditic, and often gay and lesbian experience) ... to demonstrate the possibility of collapsing boundaries of all sorts: cultural, political, patriarchal, biological."*[4]

---

[3] Cohen, 1995, p277.
[4] Ibid, p290.

Cohen is talking about academics, but his comments are equally worth bearing in mind by queer pagans.

Approaching gender in Indian contexts can, and indeed should be a daunting prospect. With over 3,000 years of literature, and over 4,000 years of material culture, there has emerged a bewildering array of positions on gender within the many Hindu traditions. As Vasudha Narayanan points out: "The discourses range from equating gender with biological sex, essentializing the 'womanly' and 'manly' characteristics, to changing behavior patterns which point to fluid gender identifications, to the rejection and transcendence of gender polarities."[5]

With thanks to Shiny Chris Hubley

[5] Narayanan, 2003, p569.

13

Multiplicious Becomings: Tantric Theologies of the Grotesque

One of the major projects I am exploring on *enfolding* is the sidling towards an (unnatural) alliance between Continental Philosophy, tantra and queer theories. An obvious point of intersection among these three areas is the emphasis on multiplicities, metamorphosis, hybridity and the grotesque.

What is the grotesque? That which is grotesque defeats attempts at easy definition. Grotesqueries inhabit a space between the known and the unknowable—their very existence questioning all modes of signification and organisation.

To confront the grotesque is to run head-on into contradiction, ambiguity, confusion—to face that which seems familiar, yet leads us astray into unknown territory; a space which cannot be ordered, or resists ordering and categorisation by its own vitality. I tend to think of 'queer' in a similar way, in the sense of queer theorists' abiding interest in undoing—on untangling the normative, questioning certainties, and dreaming alternative imaginaries. Queer is, for me, very much about committing to a resistance to easy categorisation and admitting a multitude of voices, some of which may be paradoxical and contradictory. Queer is not only about issues of gender & sexuality, but extends into questioning identity, subjectivity, embodiment. It is a call to celebrate theologies of difference.

> *"There is an entire politics of becomings-animal, as well as a politics of sorcery, which is elaborated in assemblages that are neither those of the family, nor of religion nor the State. Instead, they express minoritarian groups, or groups that are oppressed, prohibited, in revolt, or always on the fringe of recognised institutions, groups all the more secret for being extrinsic, in other words, anomic."*
> — Gilles Deleuze, Felix Guattari *A Thousand Plateaus*

I used to struggle a lot with reading Deleuze and Guattari until Patricia MacCormack advised me to treat it as *poesis,* rather than to make sense of their work. In the quote above, it is the sense of alliance with otherness that intrigues me—the notion that such alliances are a mingling, the emergence of a new kind of beingness. It points to something beyond our present categories of relation. The ways of living that have come to be identified with the rather chimeric signifier 'tantra' seethes with multiplicities and ambiguities, and to enter a tantric space requires the acceptance that whilst, at first glance, there is much that seems familiar, there is much that is different, contradictory and counter to what we might expect. Definitions of tantra abound, yet scholars and practitioners are increasingly abandoning the limitations imposed by definition and taking on board the idea of 'polythetic classification' which, rather than attempting to define tantras with a single 'essence,' allows for the examination of multiple, intersecting features. Whilst there have been a variety of attempts to come up with schema for deciding how many features a practice, text or tradition must share with others to be classed as 'tantric,' tantra remains, as Hugh Urban says, "one of the most elusive terms in the study of Asian Religions."[1] It is this elusiveness and resistance to codification which, for me, is one of the reasons why tantra is queer.

Popular representations of tantra tend to stress its supposed 'marginality'—locating it at the periphery of Hindu civic life, a practice of 'outsiders.' In this essay, I take a different tack, and examine a seemingly marginal facet of practise associated with the tantras, and show that it is, in fact, at the 'centre' of tantric life ways. That what to those outside the practice looks marginal, becomes for the devotee the centre of their orientation to the world—that the centre and the peripheral change easily shift and exchange places.

The Woman who became a ghoul

Karraikal Ammaiyar ("the Mother from Karraikal") was one of the earliest Tamil poets to write poems to Śiva. Her 143 poems, written in Tamil, point towards a world where devotees may live in the eternal presence of Śiva, and provide a window into the early development of Śaivite philosophy. Her story was hagiographised in the twelfth century *Periya Puranam*.

The woman who came to be known as Karraikal Ammaiyar was born in the 6th century CE in the coastal town of Karraikal. She was originally named Punitavati, and was married to a successful merchant named Paramatattan. She had been, from an early age, an ardent devotee of Śiva, yet she was a dutiful wife and was said to be beautiful. One day, one of Paramatattan's customers gave him two sweet mangoes, and Paramatattan ordered his wife to serve them to him for the midday meal. A Śaivite holy man came to Punitavati's house seeking alms, and she gave him one of the mangoes. When Paramatattan came to eat, Punitavati fed him and gave him the

---

[1] Urban, 2007, p3.

remaining mango. When Paramatattan called for the other mango, Punitavati prayed to Śiva for help, and a mango appeared, which she served to her husband. This mango was so delicious that Paramatattan became suspicious and asked his wife where she had obtained it. She told him, but he doubted her story and asked that she pray again to Śiva in his presence. She did so, and another mango appeared. Paramatattan took fright at this miracle, and fled from Punitavati.

Paramatattan set up another household apart from Punitavati. She continued the upkeep of his house as though he would return— he had not released her from being his wife. Eventually, Punitavati's parents found out what was going on and took their daughter to see him. Paramatattan, by this time, had taken another wife and had a daughter from her. When Punitavati appeared, they all fell at their feet and worshipped her as a goddess. When Punitavati realised that her husband did not want her as a wife, she prayed to Śiva to take away her beauty and to grant her the form of a ghoul, in order that she could devote herself entirely to the worship of Śiva in his cremation ground.

Śiva granted this boon, and she made a journey to the Himalayas. It is told that the people she met on this journey were terrified by her, but that she "converted their abhorrence to praise." She began walking on her hands, and Śiva was so moved by her devotion that he greeted her as Ammai ('mother'), and allowed her a place among his troupe of *ganas* and to eternally witness his dance.

The world as cremation ground

Karraikal Ammaiyar's transformation—from devoted wife to ghoul-devotee—shows the difference between the bounded world of the householder and that of a life lived entirely as an offering to Śiva.

This recalls an attitude to life-as-practice which can be found in later texts such as the *Saundaryalahari*:

> *"Let my idle chatter be the muttering of prayer, my every*
> *manual movement the execution of ritual gesture,*
> *my walking a ceremonial circumambulation, my eating and*
> *other acts the rite of sacrifice,*
> *my lying down prostration in worship, my every pleasure*
> *enjoyed with dedication of myself,*
> *let whatever activity is mine be some form of worship of you."[2]*

The image of Śiva in the cremation-ground, surrounded by *ganas*, ghosts, goblins and ghouls, offers a paradigm for his devotees, and the *sadhana* (practice) associated with the cremation-ground is highly prevalent in Tantra. In essence, the devotee, by practising the rites of the cremation-ground, emulates Śiva and becomes one of His family of *ganas*, or becomes Śiva and is lord of his or her own categories.

In her poetry, Ammaiyar speaks as the *pey*—the ghoul or demon *gana*—a status that is available to all devotees of Śiva, regardless of gender or caste. The cremation-ground is also frequently equated with the heart-space *(hridya)* as the seat of consciousness, and simultaneously, the site where the god's presence is felt.

Again, the theme of Śiva indwelling in the heart-space is one that can be found in later tantric texts. In Ammaiyar's poems, the world becomes the cremation-ground, for those who share in the blazing vision of Śiva.

---

[2] *The Saundaryalahari or Flood of Beauty.* W. Norman Brown. 1958. Oxford University Press. p58.

Smashan ('cremation ground practises') have been associated with early forms of tantra. These practises have received much attention in Western accounts of tantra, particularly those who prioritise its 'antinomian' nature. Consequently, there is a great deal of interest in groups such as the Aghoris and their historical forebears, the Kapalikas. Lynn Denton (2004) sees Ammaiyar as a prototypal Aghorinii: "the walking but utterly divine ghost." This is particularly interesting in respect of Ammaiyar's ability to 'convert' the abhorrence of those horrified at her appearance, which recalls the injunctions in the *Pasupata Sutra* (2nd–3rd century CE) that practitioners should "wander like a ghost" and to suffer the abuse of others, taking on their merit.

This conversion of the abhorrence of others is also a central feature of Aghori practice, and points to the liminality of the cremation ground as a place in which radical transformations take place; as such, it is a place where power may be sought. As Jonathan Parry (2004) points out, the Indian homology between body and cosmos extends to the cremation ground, which destroys the physical body, as the great fire annihilates the universe. There is a relationship between fire's destructive and creative potential, and the heat *(tapas)* generated by austerities. Cremation is also a sacrifice—a replication of the primal creative sacrifice and dismemberment of Prajapati. (Parry points to the parallels among cremation, sacrifice and birth in the *Satapatha Brahmana.)*

Despite the association with Aghoris and left-hand practises such as eating human flesh, or corpse-sitting, both Parry and Ron Barrett stress that Aghori philosophy is recognisably that of mainstream Indian liberation theology—namely that everything in creation partakes of the essence of the supreme being, Parmatma, and that all distinctions are merely superficial appearances. There is no essential difference between humanity and the divine, the auspicious and the inauspicious, the pure and the impure.

Ron Barrett's study of Aghori medicine proposes that for the Aghoris, discrimination is an illness, for which Aghori *sadhana* is the medicine. Confrontation with death is at the heart of their practice, although *smashan*-oriented practises are being supplanted by social services—educating street children and providing ashram-based care for those with socially stigmatised illnesses such as leprosy. Aghori *Śakti* ('power') is rooted in their capacity to digest—and thereby transform (via an inward assimilation)—all experiences, whether they are auspicious or inauspicious. Aghor is not a religion as it is generally understood, nor is it merely a body of practice; it is a state of mind. It is the cultivation of an attitude in which there is no aversion to anything—an attitude of nondiscrimination.[3]

Barrett is careful to point out that not all Aghoris view themselves as tantrikas, and that for Aghoris, the relationship between left-hand and right-hand path practises is more complex than the binary opposition in which they tend to be framed. For Aghoris, the *vama* and *dakshinamarge* complement each other—"like two banks of a river that work together to channel the water in a certain direction"—and that practitioners can use the methods of one path or the other, or a combination of both at different stages of his or her practice.[4]

Barrett explains that for Aghoris, the guru is considered to be the best judge for the use of left-hand practices—depending on the guru's teaching style, and the relationship between guru and disciple. Furthermore, he stresses that left-hand practises (such as consuming

---

[3] Barrett, 2008.
[4] Barrett, 2008, p152.

one's own feces) are generally considered to be temporary exercises, rather than permanent ways of living.

All ghouls together

The worlds of Karraikal Ammaiyar and contemporary Aghoris can be thought of as carnivalesque, in that their nondiscriminatory orientation to the world, their practices of engagement, suspend all hierarchies and collapse binary oppositions. As Craddock observes, Karraikal Ammaiyar's poems speak to a community of devotees where notions of caste and gender are irrelevant; all are united in the blazing vision of Śiva's dance. Their practises, so often misread as antinomian or transgressive, are celebrations of the body's capacities, a recognition of the carnality of corpses—a refusal to refute death. The woman-ghoul and the necrophagous Aghori seem to invite horror or repulsion from others, but the mistake is presumed that their practises are inspired by a wish to be repulsive, to be horrific, to assert themselves against others. Rather, Ammaiyar's becoming-ghoul, and the Aghor's embrace of the viscerality of death, point to a subjectivity not predicated on separation.

Queerying Tantras:
Bibliography

Anand, Margot. 1989. *The Art of Sexual Ecstasy: The Path of Sacred Sexuality for Western Lovers.* Jeremy P. Tarcher, Inc.

Bakhtin, Mikhail. 2009. *Rabelais and His World.* Indiana University Press.

Barrett, Ronald. 2008. *Aghor medicine: pollution, death, and healing in northern India.* University of California Press.

Berlant, Warner. 1998. *Sex in Public.*

Bhaskaran, Suparna. 2004. *Made in India: Decolonizations, Queer Sexualities, Trans/national Projects.* Palgrave Macmillan.

Carrellas, Barbara. 2007. *Urban Tantra: Sacred Sex for the Twenty-First Century.*

Cohen, Lawrence. 1995. 'The Pleasures of Castration: The Postoperative Status of Hijras, Jankhas and Academics' in Abramson, Pinkerton (eds.) *Sexual Nature/Sexual Culture.* University of Chicago Press.

Craddock, Elaine. 2007. 'The Anatomy of Devotion: The Life and Poetry of Karraikal Ammaiyar' in Pintchman, T. (ed.) *Women's Lives, Women's Rituals in the Hindu Tradition.* Oxford University Press.

Craddock, Elaine. 2010. *Śiva's Demon Devotee: Karaikkal Ammaiyar.* State University of New York.

Davidson, R.M. 2003. *Indian Esoteric Buddhism: A Social History of the Tantric Movement.* Motilal.

Deleuze, Gilles, Guattari, Felix. 1987. *A Thousand Plateaus: Capitalism and Schizophrenia.* University of Minnesota Press.

Deleuze, Gilles, Parnet, Clair. 2007. *Dialogues II.* Columbia University Press, revised edn.

Denton, Lynn Teskey. 2004. *Female Ascetics in Hinduism.* State University of New York.

Douglas, Nik; Slinger, Penny. 1979, 2000. *Sexual Secrets: The Alchemy of Ecstasy.* Destiny Books.

Feuerstein, Georg. 1998. *Tantra: The Path of Ecstasy.* Shambhala Publications Inc.

Goldberg, Ellen. 2002. *The Lord Who is Half Woman: Ardhanarishvara in Indian and Feminist Perspective.* State University of New York.

Harpham, Geoffrey G. 2007. *On the Grotesque: Strategies of Contradiction in Art and Literature.* The Davies Group Publishers.

Ingalls, Daniel. 1962. *Cynics and Pasupatas: The Seeking of Dishonor.* Harvard Theological Review. Volume 55, Issue 4.

Jagose, Annamaria. 2012. *Orgasmology.* Duke University Press.

Kramrisch, Stella. *The Presence of Śiva.* Princeton University Press, 1981.

Narayanan, Vasudha. 2003. 'Gender in a Devotional Universe', in Flood, Gavin (ed.) *The Blackwell Companion to Hinduism.* Blackwell.

Parry, Jonathan. 1994. *Death in Banaras.* Cambridge University Press.

Parry, Jonathan. 2004. 'Sacrificial Death and the Necrophagus Ascetic' in Robben (ed.) *Death, mourning, and burial: a cross-cultural reader.* Wiley.

Pattanaik, Devdutt. 2002. *The Man Who Was a Woman and Other Queer Tales from Hindu Lore.* The Haworth Press.

Thirleby, Ashley. 1982. *Tantra: The Key to Sexual Power and Pleasure.* Jaico Publishing House.

Urban, Hugh. 2003. *Tantra: Sex, Secrecy, Politics and Power in the Study of Religion.* University of California Press.

Wallis, Christopher D. 2012. *Tantra Illuminated: The Philosophy, History, and Practice of a Timeless Tradition.* Mattamayura Press.

Warner, Michael. 1991. *Fear of a Queer Planet.* University of Minnesota Press.

Warner, Michael. 2005. *Publics and Counterpublics.* Zone Books.

Three: *Queerying* Histories

As the new century opened its arms to me, I found myself increasingly intrigued by how we got to the 'now', and in particular, wanting to write about history. I would often encounter arguments and declarations on internet forums, and began to wonder where these confident assertions about the essential nature of this thing or that notion came from.

I began to be increasingly frustrated with the way that much of occult writing presents ideas and concepts as eternal, universal, cosmic laws—whereas, in actuality they all too often reflect an author's (and a moment's) particular prejudices. It is all too common in occult writing for racism or homophobia to be elevated to an unassailable plane of truth. I wanted to know, investigate and write about these notions emerging as historical processes. This seems to me to be an effective way of pulling the rug out from under them. Although I tend to regard 'Queer Paganism' as a modern innovation, I also wanted to look for eruptions of queer unruliness in different periods, and how these shaped contemporary ideas. I began to think of this doing of history as a form of resistance.

Two of the essays in this section were not originally written for *enfolding.org*. *Of Masks and Masquerades* was written in 2011 for *The Bent Pentacle*, a queer pagan blog set up by my friend Chris Hubley[1]. *Bums in Brigantia* is an old essay from 1993, one of my earliest forays into reading queerness into mythology. The title is a deliberate provocation, as there was at the time of writing, an enthusiasm for 'Celtic Shamanism' on the UK pagan scene. Doubtless its propositions are now faulty, but I simply couldn't resist including it here.

---

[1] https://thebentpentacle.wordpress.com/

14
Side Projects: Tracing Lives

A couple of years ago, prompted by a footnote in an edition of *The Logomachy of Zos* to the effect that Austin Osman Spare was one of the witnesses for the defence at the trial of Radclyffe Hall's *The Well of Loneliness* (1928), I became interested in attempting to trace this connection. Of course, none of the witnesses ever got the chance to speak, but it was interesting to think of Spare being in the same company as D.H. Lawrence, Virginia Woolf, and Vita Sackville-West. I initially speculated that Spare may have known Hall through their common interest in Spiritualism, or possibly through his friendship with the Pankhursts. It wasn't a project I devoted a lot of time to, but would bring it up occasionally whenever I ran into friends who had an interest in Spare or Hall. Dr. Ellis Saxey, who gave an enthralling lecture on Radclyffe Hall's occult interests at Treadwell's Bookshop in May 2009, reported that they were unable to find any evidence for a connection between Hall and Spare.

I often get frustrated reading biographical material about occultists as it seems to me that occult-oriented biographies focus on key individuals (and their magical ideas), but tend to leave aside relationships with other non-occulty people—or people who are considered to be 'bit players' (although, to be fair, non-occult biographers tend to downplay the magical interests/alliances of their subjects—although this is changing). Probably the most obvious example is Aleister Crowley, on whom there seems to be a great deal of focus, but relatively little concerning the other people in his life—his wives, the 'scarlet women,' his boyfriends, and his associations with various contemporaries.

Freshly back from a week in Berlin, I dropped into Treadwell's Bookshop for a chat with the owner, Christina, and she reminded me of Crowley's sojourn in Berlin in the company of Christopher Isherwood—and, in particular, an incident wherein Crowley narrowly avoided a beating during a visit to a boy-bar. Crowley had strolled up to a tough-looking young man at the bar who was wearing an open shirt, and scratched him deeply with his nails. According to Isherwood, had the young man not been given a substantial amount of money, Crowley would have been beaten up on the spot.[1]

I thought it would be interesting then, to take a brief look at the links among Crowley, Isherwood, and their contemporaries. Crowley, as is well-known, provided the basis for Isherwood's character Anselm Oakes *(A Visit to Anselm Oakes,* 1969). What emerges is a kind of Cabaret-esque Crowley—at home with the queer coterie of Isherwood and Co.

> *"The little American simply couldn't believe it. 'Men dressed as women? As women, hey? Do you mean they're queer?'*
>
> *'Eventually we're all queer,' drawled Fritz solemnly, in lugubrious tones."*

Goodbye to Berlin

Crowley arrived in Berlin in October, 1931; there was a large exhibition of his paintings at the *Nierendorff Gallery* (he had made a preliminary visit in 1930). Soon after, he met Gerald Hamilton, who was

---

[1] Fryer, 1978 p107.

then sales representative for *The Times* in Germany.[2] Hamilton is immortalised by Isherwood as the "Mr Norris" (of *Mr Norris Changes Trains*)—which Hamilton often gleefully pointed out. He seems to have shared Crowley's penchant for self-mythologising, having claimed to be the grandson of Lord Ernest Hamilton, "First Duke of Abercorn." In one of his three autobiographies—*The Way It Was With Me*—Hamilton implies that he met Isherwood at Crowley's lodgings in Berlin, but elsewhere he also states that they were already friends when they decided to call on Crowley after visiting the Nierendorff exhibition. Hamilton was the author of *Desert Dreamers* (1914, published pseudonymously)—which dealt with an Englishman's love for his young Arab guide. He had served several prison sentences (two in England, one for 'gross indecency' with another man and later, for 'unpatriotic activities'). Crowley's first mention of Isherwood is on December 25th:

> *"Big dinner; Karl, Hedy, Hamilton; later Christopher Isherwood & Stephen Spender—Bill & I both went after Hedy. Cosy Corner later—great fun with boys."*[3]

'Cosy Corner' was one of Isherwood's favourite haunts in Berlin. Hamilton became Crowley's lodger in 1932, and for a time, Crowley seems to have been enthusiastic about collaborating on a book with him about their Berlin experiences.

References to Crowley in the biographical treatments of Isherwood are sparse (I shall continue digging), although Peter Parker, in

---

[2] Diary entry 1931, p33 for Tuesday, October 13th, "Hamilton Berlin Correspondent of 'Times' called with his boy."

[3] Karl = Karl Germer; Hedy = Hedy Germer; Bill = Bertha Busch, with whom Crowley was living in Berlin.

his *Isherwood: A Life* (Picador, 2004) recounts a recollection of Jean Ross (who provided the inspiration for Isherwood's character Sally Bowles). She and Isherwood visited Crowley, only to be interrupted by the appearance of bailiffs who started removing his furniture—an incident which Isherwood also used in *Mr Norris Changes Trains*.

So far, I haven't found any references to Crowley in relation to Stephen Spender—apart from the fact that in his early years, Spender was friendly with Arthur Calder-Marshall who, as president of Oxford University Poetry Society had invited Crowley to speak— giving rise to the 'Banned Lecture' incident.

I find this sort of digging much more enjoyable than endlessly dissecting the minutiae of Crowley's magical theories.

NB: Since this essay was written, there has been some fine work done on Crowley's life and his involvement with the literary and artistic scenes of the period. In particular, Tobias Churton's *The Beast in Berlin: Art, Sex, and Magick in the Weimar Republic* (Inner Traditions, 2014). Also, Phil Baker's *City of the Beast: The London of Aleister Crowley* (Strange Attractor, 2022), and Justin Hopper's edited collection, *Obsolete Spells: Poems & Prose from Victor Neuburg & The Vine Press* (Strange Attractor, 2021).

15

Shamanism and Gender Variance: Uncovering a History

s I read through the various commentaries and observations in the wake of this year's PantheaCon[1] I came across

---

[1] In February 2011, a large Pagan conference called *Pantheacon* was held in San Jose, California. The *Pantheacon* events draw in a wide range of practitioners from various traditions. Controversy erupted following a Lilith ritual facilitated by members of the Amazon Priestess Tribe (APT), a closed group within the larger Come As You Are Coven (CAYA). Although not stated in the event's program, the ritual was intended for 'female-born women' only, and several transgender women were refused entry to the ritual space. Discussions ensued at both the event itself and across the internet. Z Budapest, one of the founders of Dianic Witchcraft, commented in response to an online discussion:

"This struggle has been going since the Women's Mysteries first appeared. These individuals selfishly never think about the following: if women allow men to be incorporated into Dianic Mysteries, what will women own on their own? Nothing! Again! Transies who attack us only care about themselves.

"We women need our own culture, our own resourcing, our own traditions.

"You can tell these are men. They don't care if women lose the Only tradition reclaimed after much research and practice, the Dianic Tradition. Men simply want in. It's their will. How dare us women not let them in and give away the ONLY spiritual home we have!"

<patheos.com/blogs/pantheon/2011/03/transgender-issues-in-pagan-religions>

people asserting that what happened was particularly reprehensible because Paganism has always been welcoming to LGBTQI people. This might well be the case in the USA, but it's certainly *not* true for the UK. It seems to me that the awareness that there are actually non-straight people who practice magic or identify as Pagans was pretty much absent from Pagan and Occult texts up until the 1990s and the occasional reference to same-sex partnerships was far outweighed by statements which tended to equate homosexuality with spiritual degeneracy and deviance. It was fairly rare to meet 'out' LGBTQI people on the 'occult scene' in the UK, and it was not unusual to find magical orders or authorities proclaiming that their groups or teachings were not open to homosexuals. That there was both a history and a vast ethnography linking gender-variance and magical practice seemingly out there, waiting to be recovered, (and of which Pagan & Occult authors seemed to be unaware), and it wasn't until the publication of books such as Will Roscoe's *Living the Spirit: A Gay American Indian Anthology* (1988), Randy Connor's *Blossom of Bone: Reclaiming the Connections Between Homoeroticism and the Sacred* (1993) and *Cassell's Encyclopedia of Queer Myth, Symbol and Spirit: Gay, Lesbian, Bisexual and Transgender Lore* (1998) that attitudes started to shift.

The controversy continued the following year, when Z Budapest announced a ritual that was intended for "genetic women" only. T. Thorn Coyle agitated for a silent protest outside the ritual space. Some participants called for a boycott of *Pantheacon* until its organizers adopted a gender-inclusive policy. For further discussion, see: Thompson, Sarah; Pond, Gina; Tanner, Philip; Omphalos, Calyxa; Polanshek, Jacobo (eds.) 2012. *Gender and Transgender in Modern Paganism*. Circle of Cerridwen Press.

On Liminal Nation[2] last year, there was a discussion regarding the perceived relationship between gender liminality and magic—particularly shamanism. This is a huge area with no easy answers (although plenty have been supplied, admittedly), but what piqued my interest was not so much that there is a relationship between people who have been identified as existing outside of the regulatory gender binary and a predisposition towards shamanism (or other magical practices), but how the two became linked as ethnographic and scientific categories.

In popular texts it's not uncommon to see this relationship between gender-variance and a predisposition towards shamanic/magical practice being treated as a transcultural universal (much in the same way as the term Shaman itself)—sometimes to the extreme that any person who identifies as LBGTQI (and any other permutation) is said to be potentially 'shamanic'—and occasionally, with the subtext that LBGTQI persons are likely to be better as shamans/magicians than straight folks. Occasionally, I've seen this argument put forward as a new and radical idea. Equally, there is the simplistic idea that the 'presence' of gender-liminal or gender-variant sacred specialists is an indication that such cultures are (or were) generally more relaxed or affirmative towards LGBTQI persons than, say, contemporary Euro-American culture.

So, I'm interested in how this (presumed) relationship between shamanism and gender-variance came about. I initially thought that the mid-nineteenth century—with the rise of both sexology (and the consequent categorisation of sexual behaviour and identities)—and the growth of the tendency to label religious specialists as hysterical or neurotic, would have been a key moment, but I've actually found

---

[2] *Liminal Nation* was an online forum, set up in 2008 by some former members of the *Barbelith* online community. It ceased operation in 2014.

that many of the tropes that we commonly encounter in contemporary discourse on shamanism (such as initiations, gender-variance, trance states, and creativity, for example), can all be found in eighteenth century writings. I do find it interesting that a great deal of contemporary writing on shamanism and its relation to sexuality still draws on eighteenth- and nineteenth-century scholarship, much of which was inherently hostile to either shamanism or gender-variance—which I mentioned in passing in my observations on *The Golden Bough* in January, 2010.[3]

For this essay series then, I'm going to examine the historical development of the relationship between shamanism and sexuality as analytical categories, and how they were related to wider cultural issues and trends. I'll start with a bit of scene-setting—examining some aspects of European attitudes to native peoples and sexual practices prior to the first wave of 'shamanic discovery' in the eighteenth century.

Noble and Ignoble Savages

Historical records which explicitly make a relationship between the religious practices of 'primitives,' 'unnatural vices,' and gender variance can be found from the sixteenth century onward. Similarly, accounts which made an explicit link between 'hermaphrodites,' sodomy and ceremonial specialisation amongst the native peoples of South America go back to the sixteenth century—and the sodomy trope was, as Michael Horswell argues, used by the Spanish to justify their conquest and conversion of the Incas. Horswell's work shows that in sixteenth century Spanish texts, a link between sodomy, effeminacy, cross-dressing and hot climates (which recurs through-

---

[3] See http://enfolding.org. This essay also appears in my collection of essays: *Hine's Varieties: Chaos & Beyond.*

out eighteenth and nineteenth century writings) was already being established.[4]

It is also from the Spanish in the sixteenth century that the first mentions of *bradaje*—later anglicised into *berdache*—can be found. They were described as effeminate or impotent men, dressed as, and performing the tasks of, women. Spanish witnesses described this behaviour as 'wicked'.[5]

Emerging European notions of 'the savage' were complex. It's not unusual to find savage peoples compared to the idealised figures of Classical mythology, and elsewhere, indiscriminately labelled as cannibals. Savages were portrayed as lacking property, religion, laws, morality or self-restraint—any feature, in fact, which Europeans thought of as essential to civilization.

Marc Lescarbot's *Histoire de la Nouvelle France* (1609) praised the Indians of New France, declaring them to be 'noble'[6].

Ter Ellingson (2001) argues that Lescarbot's work—which establishes the idea of the 'Noble Savage'—is a typical example of a European attempting to understand a different culture in terms of familiar social frameworks; that Lescarbot's assertion of savage 'nobility' was not the kind of romantic idealism one might associate with Rousseau or Hobbes, but the simple conclusion that because all the native hunted, they were—legally speaking—noble, because for Europeans, hunting was a privilege which distinguished nobles from commoners.

Travel accounts were augmented by the reports of missionaries. For example, Louis Hennepin (1640–1701), in recounting his expe-

---

[4] Horswell, 2005, p73.

[5] Gutiérrez, 2007, pp21–24.

[6] Ellingson, 2001, p22.

riences of the Mississippi Valley, describes native healers as cheats, rascals and quacks, commenting that "they never cure anyone, nor predict anything that falls out but purely by chance."[7]

Accounts of shamans trying to hinder the missionaries' work of conversion also began to appear, as well as the disappearance of shamanic practitioners in the face of advancing conversion. Neil S. Price (2001) notes that the idea that Shamanism represented a collective and widespread pattern of belief first arose when Christian missionaries in Siberia began to treat shamanic practices as a 'pagan religion' which could be overthrown.

One of the first uses of the Germanicized term 'schaman' can be found in the 1692 book *North and East Tartary* by Nicolas Witzen. Witzen's book was an account of his travels across Russia, the tribal peoples he encountered, and their "schamans" or "priests of the Devil." It was very common during the sixteenth and seventeenth centuries to see accounts of native people's religion explained in terms of devil worship or necromancy. As long as authors were careful to discuss savage peoples within the boundaries of devilish rhetoric, they were able to discuss aspects of native practices such as trances, healing or the use of narcotic substances. Samuel Purchas' 1613 work, *Purchas His Pilgrimage,* can be seen as an early attempt at comparative religion, in that Purchas reviews accounts of religious beliefs all over the world in his attempt to establish the supremacy of Anglian Christianity. Purchas' work provides an early account of a shamanic trance, and also refers to reports of "women-men" in California and Peru, and notes that "Under pretext of holiness and Religion, their principall men, on principall daies, had that hellish commerce."[8]

---

[7] Quoted in Flaherty, 1992, p31.

[8] Flaherty, 1992, p35.

Towards the end of the seventeenth century, accounts of native peoples' religious practises took an increasingly sceptical turn as the popularity of explaining any religious phenomena in rational terms developed.

16

Shamanism and Gender Variance: "Torrid Zones"

At the end of the previous essay in this series, I said I'd be taking a look at some eighteenth-century accounts of shamanism and gender-variance. Before doing so, however, I want to examine some broader transformations in the period which will, I hope, serve to place these accounts in context—specifically, discourses relating to sex, gender and human varieties (i.e., race). These transformations were inextricably linked to encounters with the peoples of the New World, and these encounters (recorded or imagined) played a formative role in the establishment of European boundaries of normative sex and gender.

"On my visit this Morning to Tynah and his Wife, I found with her a person, who altho I was certain was a Man, had great marks of effeminacy about him and created in me certain notions which I wished to find out if there were any foundations for. On asking Iddeah who he was, she without any hesitation told me he was a friend of hers, and a class of people common in Otaheite called Mahoo. That the Men had frequent connections with him and that he lived, observed the same ceremonies, and eat as the Women did. The Effeminacy of this person's speech induced me to think that he had suffered castration, and that other unnatural and shocking

148

things were done by him, and particularly as I had myself
some idea that it was common in this sea. I was however
mistaken in all my conjectures except that things equally dis-
gusting were committed."

— William Bligh, *The Log of the Bounty*, 1789

The figure of the gender-variant (male) other, which has become so central to the notion of homosexual transgression, is an image which recurs through ethnological reportage and sexological categorizations since the Enlightenment.

For now, I'm going to briefly focus on the relationship between climate and temperament—both in the New World and the Mediterranean—which came to the fore in the eighteenth century. In the first essay in this series, I noted the linkage made between climate and effeminacy. Roxanne Wheeler, in her book, *The Complexion of Race*, explains the dominant conception of human variety as rooted in the biblical account of creation—a theory of shared human origins now referred to as *monogenesis*—led to assumptions that all peoples were originally born with white skins, and that variations were due to climate and lifestyle, and that the scientific term used to designate different groups of people was 'variety' rather than 'race.' She argues that religion and clothing were significant markers of similarity and difference, and that human differences were understood mainly through the lenses of climate or humoral theories. Climactic theories of human variations became much more influential in the eighteenth century with treatises such as Montesquieu's *The Spirit of the Laws* (1748) and Samuel Smith's *Essay on the Causes of the Variety of Complexion and Figure in the Human Species* (1787). Montesquieu asserted that peoples in hot climates were prone to lively and excitable passions, which led to a state of constant arousal and immoral behaviour. This, together with physical weakness and lassitude, entailed that the people were lazy and easily enslaved due to a lack of "strength of spirit." Smith opines that all races came from a single creation, and that all subsequent racial differences are a result of climate. Savages— all of whom are, unless "urged by some violent passion," always indolent. Moreover, idleness is the cause of savagery, and a people can degenerate into a darker race, if they live in a hot climate.

The inherent idleness of savage peoples was a recurrent theme throughout the period:

> *"They are, without doubt, both in Body and Mind, the laziest People under the Sun. A monstrous Indisposition to Thought and Action runs through all the Nations of 'em: And their whole earthly Happiness seems to lie in Indolence and Supinity."*
> — Peter Kolb, *Present State of the Cape of Good-Hope* (1731)

Sarah Jordan, in *The Anxieties of Idleness,* points out that the British saw industriousness as a virtue—and rationalised their entitlement to empire on the basis that they possessed the industriousness to make proper use of the land. African idleness became a justification for slavery. Similar views were made in regard to India.

Thomas Salmon's *New Geographical and Historical Grammar* (1772) says that:

> *"The warmth of these Eastern climates has doubtless ever contributed to the indolence and effeminacy of its inhabitants; and it may be doubted whether they ever had the industry and active spirits of the inhabitants of Europe, who found the necessity of labour for their support, which the Asiatics had less occasion for, through the luxuriancy of their soil."*

Similarly, Alexander Dow's *Dissertation Concerning the Origin and Nature of Despotism in Hindostan* (1770), associates Indian hygiene and avoidance of alcohol as signs of idleness. "Habit makes the warm bath a luxury of a bewitching kind," and "The prohibition of wine is also favourable to despotism. It prevents that free communication of sentiment which awakens mankind from a torpid indifference to their natural rights."

The idea that climate could lead to degeneration and indolence for the colonisers as well as the colonised became a source of anxiety, and there were concerns that the British in India, for example, would succumb to the effeminising influences of the country, which intensified in the nineteenth century. Climactic theories persisted well into the nineteenth century—for example, in Richard Burton's infamous concept of the *Sodatic Zone* which I will examine in more depth in due course.[1]

Italian Vices

The influence of climate was not exclusively reserved for explaining the oddities of the New World. Paula Findlen's engaging account (2009) of *An Historical and Physical Dissertation on the Case of Catherine Vizzani*, edited and published by John Cleland[2] in 1751, provides some useful clues. This book, as Findlen explains, claimed to describe

"The Adventures of a young Woman, born at Rome, who for eight years passed in the Habit of a Man, was killed for an Amour with a young Lady; and being found, on Dissection, a

---

[1] I still haven't gotten around to doing this.
[2] Cleland is best-remembered for his *Fanny Hill: or, the Memoirs of a Woman of Pleasure.*

*true Virgin, narrowly escaped being treated as a Saint. With
some Curious and Anatomical Remarks on the Nature and
Existence of the Hymen."*

Despite the lurid possibilities of a tale of sex between women,
cross-dressing, and the peculiarities of the Italians, the book was not,
apparently, a success. At the end of the volume, Cleland expresses the
climatic view of Italy: "In a warm country like theirs, where Impuri-
ties of all Sorts are but too frequent, it may well happen that such
strange Accidents may, from Time to Time, arise as highly to excite
both their Wonder and their Attention." The climatic values: laxity
of morals, indolence and religious transgressions were applied to Italy
(and France, to a lesser extent), and the popularity of the Grand Tour
led to increased anxieties about the effects on British moral values.

The anonymous author of *Reasons for the Growth of Sodomy in
England* (1729) proferred the view that Italy was the "mother and
nurse of sodomy," and linked the growth of sodomy to the growing
popularity in England of Italian opera. Similar anxieties were
expressed concerning the popularity of masquerade balls (see Essay
20).

17

Shamanism and Gender Variance: Two Sexes, Three Genders?

"Among the women I saw some men dressed like women, with whom they go about regularly, never joining the men. The commander called them amaricados, perhaps because the Yumas call effeminate men maricas. I asked who these men were, and they replied that they were not men like the rest, and for this reason they went around covered in this way. From this I inferred that they must be hermaphrodites but from what I learned later I understood that they were sodomites, dedicated to nefarious practices. ...I conclude that in this matter of incontinence there will be much to do when the Holy Faith and the Christian religion are established among them."

— Fray Pedro Font, *Font's Complete Diary of the Second Anza Expedition 1775–1776*

For this essay, I'm going to briefly summarise some themes in contemporary scholarship relating to eighteenth-century attitudes to sex and gender which underwent great changes throughout the period. This is useful for understanding eighteenth-century accounts of shamanism, as many of these accounts throughout the century increasingly focused on what we would now call 'gender-variance' as a marker for shamanic behaviour. Several scholars have argued that due to changes in the way sexuality and gender were understood in eighteenth-century European culture, contact accounts of primitive cultures shifted towards an increased focus upon same-sex desires as a special case—that of the 'effeminate sodomite.' Whereas prior notions of 'sodomy' included both men and women, and partners both active and passive, a new sexual theory arose that equated cross-gender roles with femininity and passivity.[1]

From one sex to two sexes?

The central argument of Thomas Laqueur's *Making sex: body and gender from the Greeks to Freud* (1990) is that the understanding of the relationship between men and women underwent a major transformation over the course of the eighteenth century.

Prior to this transformation, a 'one-sex model' was the dominant scheme, based on the idea that the body was composed of four humours—cold, hot, moist and dry—and that men were dominantly composed of hot and dry humours, and women by cold and moist humours. Another key element was that differences of sex were differences of degree. Semen, for example, was produced by bodily heat, and it was thought that women with too much bodily heat could produce semen, and even, if they became too hot through excessive exercise, suddenly develop a penis! Menstruation was similarly understood not as something unique to women, but as an example of the body's propensity to bleed to expel excess materials. Only one body existed, and it was represented as essentially male; and whilst females were thought of as 'lesser males' with outside-in bodies, men and women

---

[1] See Bleys, 1996, p81.

were not considered to be radically different in terms of bodily constitution. Medical literature conceptualised the female body as an 'inferior' version of the male body, with equivalences between testicles and ovaries; scrotum and uterus; foreskin and labia. Some physicians believed that men's genitalia were externalised due to the heat of male bodies, which 'drove' their organs outwards. Metaphysical understandings of the hierarchy of nature made men and women part of the same order, with men placed above women. However, whilst women becoming men due to excess heat was accepted, the notion that men could become women was not. This was due to the belief that nature tended towards perfection, and for a man to become a woman would be unnatural—the perfect becoming imperfect. Laqueur argues that during the eighteenth century, this 'one-sex model' was replaced by a 'two-sex model' in which men and women became anatomically opposites, radically different from each other, and hierarchically divided.[2]

Laqueur proposes that the 'two-sex model' emerged primarily due to political changes and the decline of religious authority, and not to medical discoveries. Laqueur proposes that to reinforce the political notion of natural rights, bodies were redefined in terms of opposite sexes. Power could only be formally granted to one group (men) and withheld from another group (women) if the two were distinct and incommensurable—and political theorists turned to biology and medical treatises to justify this view in terms of emerging scientific discourse, rather than Adam's dominance over Eve. So, for example, the demotion of the pre-Enlightenment metaphysical order took place at the same time as the fragmentation of social order, and the remaking of the human body was intrinsic to changes in the political,

---

[2] Laqueur, 1990, pp5–6.

social and economic spheres—ranging from the development of the factory system and its division of labour, to the changes brought about by the French Revolution.[3]

There is some debate amongst scholars over the timing of this shift to the 'two-sex model,' with some historians locating the beginning of the shift in the sixteenth and seventeenth century, whilst others have pointed out that this process was also historically uneven, with the single-sex and two-sex frameworks continuing to exist side-by-side for some time. Despite critiques, however, Laqueuer's work has had a considerable impact on contemporary studies of sexuality & gender.

Mollies: a third gender?

Randolph Trumbach, in his book, *Sex and the Gender Revolution*, proposes that from around 1700, there appeared a subculture of adult males whose desires were exclusively directed to adult and adolescent males. These men were identified by their fellows by virtue of their effeminate mannerisms, speech and modes of dress. He argues that for most of the eighteenth century, there existed an understanding of three genders—men, women and sodomites.[4]

According to Trumbach, prior to the eighteenth century in European societies, same-sex desire between males was organised around differences in age, between active, adult men and passive youths—a pattern, which he points out, was present in ancient Greece and Rome, and in early Christian Europe and the later Middle Ages. Trumbach cites the work of Michael Rocke (see *Forbidden Friendships*) in demonstrating that in Renaissance Florence, sodomy was nigh on universal between men, but always structured by age. Trumbach points out that although sodomy was illegal, and the

---

[3] Laqueur, 1990, p11.
[4] Trumbach, 1998, p3.

church spoke out against it as immoral, "the actual sexual behaviour of men had changed very little from what it had been in the ancient pagan Mediterranean world."

From the 1690s onwards, opinion changed from the old system—which was characterised by all males passing through a period of sexual passivity in adolescence—to a new system, wherein sexual passivity and homosexual desire was presumed to be indicative of an effeminate minority. These 'new' adult sodomites were known colloquially as *mollies*—a term which, Trumbach says, was first applied to female prostitutes, and were characterized, he argues, by playing two roles—one in the public world and another in the so-called 'molly-house' inside which they took women's names and adopted the speech and body movements of women. Historians have uncovered a well-established network of molly-house and open-air meeting places distributed throughout London in the early eighteenth century. In addition to Mother Clap's molly-house in Holborn, there were also houses near the Old Bailey and Newgate Prison, in Soho, Charing Cross, Drury Lane, and St. James's Square. A pamphlet attacking Charles Hitchins, a prominent thief-taker in London in the 1710s, described the behaviour inside a molly-house: men calling one another 'my dear,' and hugging, kissing and tickling each other...and assuming effeminate voices and airs. Some were dressed up as milkmaids or shepherdesses, whilst others wore the latest women's fashions, such as extensive hoop petticoats.[5]

Mollies became the focus of increased public scrutiny and condemnation, and some historians have argued that the Societies for the Reformation of Manners, which attacked effeminate sodomites in print, helped forge a link between the flouting of codes of masculine

---

[5] Hitchcock, 1997, p68.

behaviour with the idea that such men were exclusively interested in sex with other men. These societies were concerned with social reform, particularly the elimination of blasphemy, idleness and lewd and disorderly behaviour. They frequently relied on informers and agents to gather evidence, and although their most frequent targets were prostitutes, it is their attacks on molly houses (1699, 1707 and 1726) which has provided much of the historical evidence for the existence of molly culture. The Societies published trial reports, public sermons and accounts of their own activities, and from the late 1690s onwards, there were frequent references to both molly-houses and sodomites in printed pamphlets and newspapers. Hitchcock points out that whilst the Reformation Societies closed down molly-houses, those men who were publicly exposed on the pillory were sometimes savagely treated by the London crowd—many were severely injured and some men died.

Men displaying effeminate mannerisms were increasingly subject to blackmail, persecution and punishment, and it is argued that the increased emphasis on legal regulation also contributed to the idea that the sodomite was a distinct social and sexual type. Prior to the eighteenth century, the term 'sodomite' encompassed a wide range of acts, but by the early eighteenth-century, it came to denote almost exclusively sexual acts between men. Trumbach discusses that many boys and men charged with sodomy were represented at their trials as 'mollies' (regardless of whether or not they exhibited signs of effeminacy), and suffered the stigma and the harsh punishments associated with such an attribution. Such developments, he contends, obliged men to present their masculine status exclusively through their interest in women—and sex ceased to be represented as that which took place between an active and passive partner (regardless of gender), but as an act between men and women.

As the eighteenth century progressed, sodomy and effeminacy came under increasing scientific scrutiny. Some social theorists interpreted same-sex desire as being produced by luxury, excess and idleness—an explanation which pointed not only to modern European cultures, but also 'primitive' societies (see the previous essay for some related discussion). The sailor, John Marra, for example, in his *Journal of the Resolution's Voyage in 1772, 1773, 1774 and 1775 on Discovery in the Southern Hemisphere* (published in London in 1775) described the Polynesians as "an effeminate race, intoxicated with pleasure, and enfeebled by indulgence."[6] Effeminacy could also be a product of cultures where men spent too much time around women, or as John Millar theorised, societies where women had too much political or social status.

---

[6] Wilson, 2004, p351.

18

Reincarnation and 'Uranian' Souls in the Nineteenth Century

I t often seems to me that many occult representations of gender are rooted in nineteenth-century formations, so I thought it'd be interesting to examine some occult theories that emerged in this period. These theories included representations of the connection made between reincarnation, masculinity & femininity, and the soul's evolution. There is also the influence of the so-called 'Uranian' temperament which emerged from various Theosophical sources in the late nineteenth & early twentieth century.

Reincarnation was a central tenet of Theosophical doctrine, and many Theosophists believed that experiencing male and female bodies through reincarnation and the different lessons learned thereof, was necessary for long-term spiritual development. Some teachings took for granted the naturalness of distinctions between masculine & feminine temperaments, although they tended towards the view that any such distinctions were 'temporary' in that the fully spiritualised soul was 'above' sex—a divine hermaphrodite or androgyne. Some Theosophists argued that there were male and female souls, and that the physical body reflected the nature of the indwelling soul, whilst others claimed that the Higher Self was neither one nor the other, but shared the characteristics of both. These representations of the relationship between masculine & feminine temperaments were also contested and modified by women who combined esoteric beliefs with a feminist outlook.

In 1890, Susan E. Gay published a Theosophical-Feminist Manifesto in the Theosophical Journal *Lucifer*. Gay asserted that souls reincarnated in both male and female bodies, gaining the "noble qualities" of both sexes gradually, and that the ideal was a condition of "spiritual equilibrium"—the exemplar being Jesus. Gay asserts that "manly men" or "womanly women" were the least developed of souls, and she believed that if men realised that at some point in the future, they might find themselves incarnated in female physical bodies; and then this might cause them to think twice about their assumptions that women were 'naturally' subordinate to men. Gay argued that men had to disabuse themselves of the notion that:

> *"physical manhood is a sort of freehold possession to be held here and hereafter, which marks off certain souls from certain others known as women, and confers on them all sorts of superior rights and privileges, including the possession and submission of 'wives.'"*[1]

A much more radical feminist theology of the soul was that expounded by Frances Swiney. In *The Awakening of Women* (1899), Swiney asserted that all souls were essentially feminine, and although they had to progress through a 'masculine' state, this was but a 'kindergarten' period. Drawing on a wide array of theories, from biological arguments to Kabbalah, Swiney conceived of Christ as a woman who had sacrificed herself for humanity by taking on a 'lower' form—a male. Whilst calling for an improvement in women's economic and social conditions, Swiney also believed that men would

---

[1] Gay, 1890, pp121–122.

eventually become obsolete. Woman, for Swiney, was Nature, and man's mistake was in living apart from all that is 'natural.'

> *"The degeneracy we deplore lies at the door*
> *of a selfish, lustful, diseased manhood."*[2]

If this view seems somewhat extreme to modern eyes, we should recall that Darwin, in *The Descent of Man,* had stated quite plainly that men's superiority to women was a direct consequence of evolution, and scientists such as Gustav Le Bon and Karl Vogt had both 'demonstrated' that women were closer to apes, in terms of cranial capacity. Swiney founded "The League of Isis" which crusaded against prostitution, incest and sexual abuse. A strong believer in eugenics, Swiney believed that "sexual restraint" would lead to "racial improvement" by limiting the numbers of children born, and ensuring that those children that were born received better care.

The idea that the soul changed sex—to learn lessons and evolve—also became a key theme in Charles Webster Leadbeater's view of reincarnation. He asserted that the soul stayed incarnated as one sex for 3–7 lives before changing to the other, although there were exceptions where more advanced souls would be reborn into the sex and race which were best suited for the soul's development. In 1898, Leadbeater and Annie Besant collaborated in an occult investigation of the past lives of a Miss Annie Wilson, Mrs Besant's secretary and housekeeper. *The Lives of Arcor,* as this work came to be known, traced Miss Wilson's past lives from as far back as 60,000 years before the birth of Christ. A theme that emerges in *The Lives of Arcor,* and recurs in other reincarnatory genealogies that Leadbeater produced, is that individuals who work together as Theosophists in their present

---

[2] Swiney, 1907, p43.

lives have had close relationships in the past, usually involving changes of sex. It was revealed, for example, that in one incarnation, Miss Wilson had been Annie Besant's son, and in another, some 60,000 years later in China, had been her wife. A later work of Leadbeater's, *The Lives of Alcyone,* which traced the many past lives of Krishnamurti, caused shock and outrage in Theosophical circles when it revealed that Leadbeater had, in previous incarnations, been married to Krishnamurti and his brother, and that Christ, in a previous incarnation, had been married to Julius Caesar.

One Theosophist who made connections between Leadbeater's theories of reincarnation and current developments in sexology was Charles Lazenby. Lazenby held a degree in psychology and later studied Jungian psychoanalysis, and was a close friend of both Havelock Ellis and Edward Carpenter. Lazenby accepted Leadbeater's assertion that the soul 'changes sex' every seven incarnations, but opined that the soul has six lives which are wholly masculine or feminine, and that for the seventh life, the masculine soul "takes on the colouring of the feminine" (and, presumably, *vice versa*)—and that the purely masculine or feminine soul is found only at the midpoint of each cycle of lives. Later in life Lazenby associated this transitional incarnation with the notion of the "intermediate sex," and used the term 'Uranian' to denote individuals whose physical bodies belonged to one sex, yet whose thoughts and desires belonged to the other.

The term 'Uranian' had been coined in the 1860s by the German Karl Heinrich Ulrichs, who used "Uranian" (frequently Germanised as *Urning*) to signify those who experienced "a congenital reversal of sexual feeling." 'Uranian' was also a term much used in astrological and esoteric circles—usually in reference to the planet Uranus, which was associated with "awakening the soul from lethargy, and bringing it into strange conditions and hazardous enterprises." Esoterically, at the time, the influence of Uranus was very much bound up with the idea that human culture was entering a New Age. In Theosophical writings, the term 'Uranian' began to denote a new human type—unconventional, spiritually advanced, and a blend of masculine & feminine temperaments.

An underlying theme in the debates over sexuality, morality and occultism was the relationship between sexuality and religion. In the emerging sexology of the period, there was a connection between spiritual experience and sexual mania. There was also a connection being advanced between spirituality and homosexuality. Both Havelock Ellis and Edward Carpenter argued that there was an organic relationship between spiritual development and the "homosexual temperament." This, according to Ellis in *Sexual Inversion* (1897), was reinforced by anthropological studies which confirmed the "aptitude of the invert for primitive religion, for sorcery and divination." Carpenter went further in his 1919 book, *Intermediate Types Among Primitive Folk,* arguing that there was a direct connection between the blending of masculine and feminine temperaments which gave rise to "inverts," and the development of psychic or unusual powers. Those who were of the "intermediate sex," Carpenter asserted, overcame the purely masculine or feminine, combining the strengths of both:

> *"It may also point to a further degree of evolution than usually attained and a higher order of consciousness, very imperfectly realised, but indicated. This interaction, in fact, between the masculine and the feminine, this mutual illumination of logic and intuition, this combination of action and meditation, may not only raise and increase the power of each of these faculties, but it may give the mind a new quality ... It*

may possibly lead to the development of that third order of perception which has been called the cosmic consciousness, and which may also be termed divination."[3]

Carpenter's view of 'inversion' as a sign of spiritual evolution rather than aberration would be taken up later by Weimar-era German publications such as *Die Freundschaft* which promoted same-sex love and romantic friendship in both political and spiritual terms.

Whilst some Theosophists accepted the ideal of an 'intermediate sex' as part of the approaching New Age—or at least the idea that humanity would be hermaphroditic—it tended to be couched in terms of human beings no longer having sex-organs or having to go through the whole sordid business of reproduction—very much in keeping with the asexual coming together of souls that permeated a good deal of theosophical writings. Theosophists, whilst apparently willing to discuss the divine hermaphrodite as an ideal, could not accept same-sex activity on the 'physical' plane.

---

[3] Carpenter, 1919, p63.

19

Polarity: The Early Evolution of a Concept

I t is not unusual to see arguments for polarity supported by exhortations to think how polarity 'works' in terms of electricity, magnetism or the generic, all-encompassing term, 'energy.' My contention here is that the explanations of sex/gender polarity that are underwritten by appeals to 'energies' of various kinds did not pop out of nowhere, and that, despite ahistorical appeals to esoteric tradition or the energy systems of 'ancient cultures,' the roots of these discourses can be traced back to concepts which emerged in the eighteenth and nineteenth centuries.

Of particular importance are the influence of developments in electricity, thermodynamics, and the technologies of the industrial revolution, all of which led to new understandings of the body as an energetic system.

The eighteenth century was a period of rapid social & political change, over the course of which, due to a wide variety of factors, the pre-Enlightenment (Aristotelian) view that women were 'inferior men' shifted towards the recognisably 'modern' view that men and women were different sexes. This did not happen in a neatly linear fashion, nor was this primarily because of the advance of scientific discoveries, but rather in social and political changes which laid the groundwork for the naturalisation of the concept that men and women were incommensurably opposite and that gender was biological.

During the eighteenth century, electrical discoveries and applications came very swiftly. The first incandescent light bulb was made in 1709. In 1733, Dufray postulated that there were two types of electricity—resinous and vitreous. In 1730, Stephen Grey performed the first electrical experiment on a human being, electrifying a young boy. This led to a rise in the electrification of human beings as both entertainment and educational spectacle. One of the most popular demonstrations was the 'electrifying Venus' invented by G.M. Bose, in which a woman stood on an insulated stool while an operator charged her body with an electrical machine. Men in the audience were invited to kiss her, but would be discouraged by a strong spark.

Bose produced an explanation of electrical phenomena based on a distinction between male and female electric fire—the male fire was strong and powerful and visibly manifested as sparks; whilst the female fire was a weak, luminous emanation—the kind of light that characterised the aurora borealis. Charles Rabiqueau viewed sexual reproduction as an electrical process—the ovaries being "inert and lifeless: like an unlit candle or an egg ready to receive the spark of life."

Electricity, over the course of eighteenth century, became a force that connected bodies and minds; its power was linked to sexuality and passion, and the discoveries fueled both theological and rational speculation about universal forces.

In the early part of the nineteenth century, electricity was thought to be the force most likely to prove the existence of the *élan vitale*— the life force of Naturalphilosophie. Schelling, at the turn of the century, for example, proposed that heat, light, magnetism and electricity were all byproducts of a single universal life force. The arising of electrical models allowed polarities to be discovered within organisms, and between discrete classes of persons. Thus, maleness or masculinity was assigned to the positive pole, and femininity to the negative. The gendering of electricity and energy continued in the nineteenth century, particularly in respect to medical theories and the notion of 'nervous energy.' Electrical theory was also wheeled out in support of the widespread belief that women, whilst mentally and physically inferior to men, were more 'sensitive.' In 1844, Baron Charles Von Reichenbach experimented with 'feeble-brained' teenage girls, placing them in a darkened room and then exposing them to magnets. Reichenbach concluded that girls possessing a "diseased sensibility" could perceive a flickering aura around magnets. Reichenbach went on to develop a theory of "Odic force" which pervaded all matter—and that proper alignment with the Earth's polarity could prevent illness. (Reichenbach's theories are still being drawn on today as evidence for the scientific recognition of occult energies.)

By the middle of the nineteenth century, doctors were warning of the dangers of a depleted nervous system; over-exertion, could sap an individual's reserves of nervous energy, and could lead to depression, fatigue or melancholia. Nervous energy was often described in the terminology of economics or physics. For example, the American physician, George Beard, who coined the term "neurasthenia" in 1881, described sufferers as under-charged batteries—and the cause of neurasthenia was not moral lapses, but the pressures of modern civilisation caused by the new technologies of steam power, the telegraph, and the popular press. Women, as the weaker gender, thought Beard, were more likely to succumb to the stresses of modern life. Women were particularly susceptible if they tried to imitate men by seeking 'excessive' education or intellectual efforts which depleted their store of nervous energy.

The concept of nervous energy was used both by doctors to account for female weaknesses, and following the surge of interest in Spiritualism in the 1840s, by Spiritualists themselves in accounting for the particular suitability of women as mediums. Spiritualists, in attempting to distance themselves from charges of superstition, drew on current scientific theories and popular understandings of current technologies (such as the telegraph) for their accounts of spirit phenomena. One explanation, for example, of why women were particularly suitable as mediums, was their very weaknesses in the masculine qualities of will and intelligence, and their feminine qualities of passivity and impressionability. Another was that women's 'negative charge' attracted spirits which were 'positively charged.' Whilst women were routinely distinguished from men due to their powers of intuition or imagination, these seemingly positive traits were produced because women were weak-willed and unable to reason intellectually. Some Spiritualists believed that a woman's abundance (or imbalance) of nervous energy made her more receptive to the higher electro-magnetic transmissions of the spirits, whilst doctors felt that this same imbalance led to ailments—considering the body as a great telegraphic network which, overtaxed by the unstable currents flowing through it, responded with hysteria and mania.

The dominant view of 'respectable' Victorian womanhood was underwritten by the 'natural' assumption that women were innately passive and fragile, whilst men were rational, active and possessed will-power. Man's sphere was the public world; woman's sphere the home and domestic life. This view was upheld both by religious authorities and by scientists, doctors and educationalists. Whilst clerics invoked Biblical proofs, scientists turned to biology. Victorian science, although it portrayed itself as objective and disinterested, was underwritten by cultural prejudices and by 'common sense,' and this is particularly obvious for pronouncements on women's abilities. In the nineteenth century, the 'common sense' assertion that men were rational and intellectual, and women were emotional and intuitive was reinforced through scientific pronouncements that irrefutably demonstrated a biologically determined difference between the sexes. Darwin, for example, makes this distinction very clear in *The Descent of Man* (1871):

> *"The chief distinction in the intellectual powers of the two sexes is shown by man's attaining to a higher eminence, in whatever he takes up, than can woman—whether requiring deep thought, reason, or imagination, or merely the use of the senses and hands. If two lists were made of the most eminent men and women in poetry, painting, sculpture, music (inclusive both of composition and performance), history, science, and philosophy, with half a dozen names under each subject, the two lists would not bear comparison."*[1]

Scientific proofs that men were rational and women emotional (and deficient in the capacity for logical thought) indirectly supported the view that women and men were complementary to each other (and therefore, women should not attempt to 'compete' with men). The anthropologist J. McGrigor Allan, in 1869, asserted that: "In reflective power, woman is utterly unable to compete with man," and that woman "is content, in most instances, to let others think for her...and discover the most proper person to do so." Allan believed that efforts to educate women would be useless; that "Any encroachment of one sex on the physical and mental characteristics of the other, is unnatural and repulsive..." and pointed to differences in

---

[1] Darwin, 1871, p327.

biology which "predisposes men for intellectual and women for reproductive work," adding that "the history of humanity is conclusive as to the mental supremacy of the male sex."[2] One element of the 'proof' of women's mental inferiority came from comparisons of brain size. Allan explained that "the female skull approaches in many respects that of the infant, and still more that of the lower races." Craniologist and early crowd psychologist Gustave Le Bon concurred:

"In the most intelligent races, as among the Parisians, there are a large number of women whose brains are closer in size to those of gorillas than to the most developed male brains. This inferiority is so obvious that no one can contest it for a moment; only its degree is worth discussion. All psychologists who have studied the intelligence of women, as well as poets and novelists, recognize today that they represent the most inferior forms of human evolution and that they are closer to children and savages than to an adult, civilized man.

"They excel in fickleness, inconstancy, absence of thought and logic, and incapacity to reason. Without doubt there exist some distinguished women, very superior to the average man, but they are as exceptional as the birth of any monstrosity, as, for example, of a gorilla with two heads; consequently, we may neglect them entirely."[3]

---

[2] Quoted in Murphy, 2006, p15.

[3] Le Bon 'Recherches Anatomiques et Mathematiques sur les Lois des Variations du Volume du Cerveau et sur leurs Relations avec l'intelligence', *Revue d'anthropologie*, 1879.

Le Bon also weighed in against the ideas that women could be educated, and were capable of competing in male activities:

> *"A desire to give them the same education, and, as a conse-quence, to propose the same goals for them, is a dangerous chimera... The day when, misunderstanding the inferior occupations which nature has given her, women leave the home and take part in our battles: on this day, a social revo-lution will begin, and everything that maintains the sacred ties of the family will disappear."*[4]

Influential physicians such as Henry Maudsley argued that not only should women's education be limited to their "foreordained" work as mothers and nurses of children, but that excessive mental strain would lead to "physical degeneration" and lead to future racial decay.

Spiritualist literature often portrayed women in terms of this ideal. It was woman's passivity—her innate 'finer feelings'—which, for spiritualists, allowed women to become effective mediums. As Alex Owen (2004) explains, women's passivity, which was widely con-strued as restricting their ability to function in the public sphere, became synonymous for Spiritualists with power.

Some spiritualists believed that one did not choose to become a medium—one was effectively chosen by the spirits—and the devel-opment of a medium's abilities was guided by the spirits, rather than the individual. In spiritualist discourse, the very qualities which made women appear to be deficient (when set against the norms of mascu-line qualities) rendered them as effective mediums—the delicate constitutions and heightened nervous sensitivity. The passivity and

---

[4] Ibid.

impressionability which women had, became the markers of a successful capacity for contacting spirits. (NB: This theme of passivity as a primary qualification for mediumship was one of the reasons why Madame Blavatsky disassociated herself from the spiritualist movement). William B, Potter's 1865 work *Spiritualism As It Is*, for example, continually stresses the importance of sustaining a "passive or negative relation to the intelligences who seek to impress us..."

Such passivity—although natural for women—led to suspicions of "unmanly behaviour" for male mediums. The poet Robert Browning, for example, dismissed the celebrated medium D.D. Home as "effeminate" and a "sot" and later lampooned all mediums (especially Home) in a poem entitled "Mr. Sludge, the Medium". Medical detractors of spiritualism often linked it to hysteria—and hysteria in men was thought to be indicative of, as John Russell Reynolds put it in his *A System of Medicine* (1879), a sign that men were "either mentally or morally of feminine constitution."[5] Medical pronouncements of the symptoms of hysteria portrayed such women in terms of degeneracy, waywardness and willfulness—some directly equating spiritualism with "emotional incontinence." An American physician, Frederick Marvin, describing the condition of "utromania" (a disease brought on by a mis-angled womb), stated that sufferers were susceptible to "embrace some strange ultra 'ism'—Mormonism, Mesmerism, Fourierism, Socialism, often Spiritualism."[6]

Polarity was given a further scientific boost with the arrival of thermodynamics. As nineteenth-century physics advanced, it generated new metaphors for the body; the view of the previous century of the body as *l'homme machine*—in which the body was essentially mech-

---

[5] Reynolds, 1868, p307.
[6] Quoted in Owen, 2004, p149.

anistic and engineered—was replaced by that of the 'human motor.' The body was conceived of as an engine—with its own internal fuel reservoir—regulated by internal principles (including internal self-motivation), and converting that fuel into heat, and thence into physical work. There was a great effort to quantify, measure and instrumentalise the body's energies, in the hope of achieving perfection. As a motor, the human body was frequently compared to a steam engine—sometimes with the brain acting as an 'engineer'—and 'nerve force' came to occupy a kind of middle ground between the insubstantial mind and the forces of nature. The principle of the first law of thermodynamics—energy conservation—was used to explain that the 'energy' women expended in reproduction meant that they lacked the reserves for any other purpose. Herbert Spencer (1873), for example, claimed that there was a "somewhat earlier arrest of individual evolution in women than in men, necessitated by the reservation of vital power to meet the cost of reproduction." Patrick Geddes' and J. Arthur Thompson's *The Evolution of Sex* (1889) argued that maleness and femaleness were differentiated down to the level of cellular metabolism. Men were thus active, energetic and variable, whilst women were sluggish, passive and conservative. Geddes was not in favour of women's suffrage: "What was decided among the prehistoric protozoa cannot be annulled by Act of Parliament."

Similarly, in 1891, the psychologist Harry Campbell proclaimed that women were not only "less intellectual" than men, but that the "emotional and intellectual portions" of men and women are "somewhat in inverse ratio." There were dissenters, notably the botanist Lydia Becker and Antoinette Brown Blackwell, who declared in 1870, "I find nothing in physiology which indicates that the woman's intellect is organically inferior to the man's intellect,"[7] and stressed the importance of environmental influences. Nevertheless, the belief that thermodynamics and biology 'proved' the inevitability of the 'separate spheres' of women and men, became dominant. Darwin, Galton and the influential physician Henry Maudsley, for example, asserted that differences between the sexes were innate, and that education and environment have little effect, if any. The argument was extended further in biological terms, with the notion that women's nervous systems were less well developed than men's, as were their brains. Also, it was frequently asserted that women's (and 'savages') purported ability to withstand discomfort 'stoically' was an indication of their 'lower development.'

The law of energy conservation was also used to argue against women's education. It was frequently asserted that, since the human body had a finite supply of energy which had to be carefully regulated, educating women would place them under undue "mental strain" which would be injurious to their health. A physician, T.S. Clouston, in discussing the dangers of education for women asserted: "If you use the force of your steam-engine for generating electricity, you cannot have it for sawing your wood."[8] referring to the view that women's bodies were biologically and energetically concerned with reproduction and nurturance, and nothing else. Similarly, William Acton (1857) argued that women were indifferent to sex and that this was entirely natural, to "prevent the male's vital energies from being overly expended at any one time," whilst other medical men, such as Henry Maudsley, defined women entirely in terms of their "reproductive functions." Not only was education a danger for women as

---

[7] Quoted in Murphy, 2006, p18.
[8] Clouston, 1883, p216.

individuals, but it also threatened the future development of the race, and there were frequent claims that women's intellectual advancement would lead to them becoming "unsexed," and uninterested in continuing the human species.

20

Of Masks and Masquerades

Going to a masked ball to flounce, flaunt and flirt is a well-established feature of contemporary London life, and whether a private or public event, does not occasion much comment. However, in the eighteenth century, when masquerades first became popular public events, it was a very different matter. Masquerades were scandalous events which, according to their detractors, threatened the very social fabric of the land.

Masquerades as commercial, public entertainments became popular in England in the 1720s. More English people were travelling abroad, and as a consequence, there was a rise in interest in the traditional carnivals and sophisticated masquerades of the Continent. One of the first promoters of masquerades in London was the 'Swiss Count' John Heidegger, who organised 'Midnight Masquerades' at the Haymarket Theatre; these attracted up to eight hundred people per week. By the 1770s, some masquerade events had as many as two thousand attendees.

Although masquerades were a public, ticketed event, they quickly gained a reputation for debauchery and licentious behaviour. In eighteenth-century novels, the masquerade is frequently used as a setting for scenes of adultery and seduction. Masks were commonly thought to heighten erotic attraction, and the wearing of masks was associated with prostitutes. Also, masks liberated their wearers from the strictures of decorum and moral restraint, and donning a mask was thought to make the wearer sexually uninhibited (particularly women). Costumes, too, could be scandalous. Whilst popular themes for costumes represented stock characters such as shepherdesses, perriots, hussars, punches and harlequins, mythical figures such as the goddess Diana, the Queen of the Fairies, dragons, satyrs, pans and wood-woses were sometimes used. An account of a masquerade in 1773 reports the appearance of a Green Man "in a very fanciful dress, all covered with leaves of ivy." In 1749, one Miss Chudleigh (later the Duchess of Kingston) shocked onlookers by appearing as a bare-breasted Iphigenia. Some costumes represented 'wayward' nuns and priests—a common theme in eighteenth-century erotic literature. In Charles Johnson's *The Masquerade* (1719), Lady Frances says, "I will appear in all the gloomy inaccessible charms of a young devotee; there is something in this character so sweet and forbidden."

But it was cross-dressing—women dressed as beaux or hussars and men as witches, bawds and shepherdesses—which caused particular outrage. As a writer in the *Universal Spectator* (1728) put it: "In every country, Decency requires that the sexes should be differenc'd by Dress, in order to prevent multitudes of Irregularities which otherwise would continuously be occasion'd." The author of *Short Remarks Upon the Original and Pernicious Consequences of Masquerades* averred that the appearance of cross-dressing men at masquerades was making England "a very Sodom for Lewdness"; and naming infamous cross-dressers from antiquity—such as Caligula or Heliogabalus who were "the Scum, the Scandal and the Shame of Mankind"—warned that masquerades were modern imitations of ancient pagan perversity. Terry Castle (1986) argues that the masquerade, particularly in literature, allowed forbidden or transgressive forms of behaviour such as homosexuality or incest to appear—as long as they are unintentional or accidental consequences of the confusion and chaos engendered by the disguise and anonymity offered by the masquerade. In John Cleland's 1749 *Memoirs of a Woman of Pleasure* (a.k.a. *Fanny Hill)* a prostitute named Emily, attending a masquerade disguised as a boy, is approached by a "handsome domino" who begins to pay her attention. At first, she finds his courtship "dashed with a certain oddity," but it becomes clear that the man "took her really for what she appeared to be, a smock-faced boy" (i.e., a feminine-looking boy). The pair go off to a nearby *bagnio* (bath-house) where the man—although somewhat disappointed to find that Emily is not a boy—attempts to sodomise her, and she has to redirect him "down the right road."

Masquerades were also associated with the emerging character of the 'Sodomite.' In one of the popular histories of the notorious criminal Jonathan Wild (hanged at Tyburn in 1725), there is an account of a masquerade attended by "He-whores" at a "Sodomitish Academy" which Gerald Howson (2006) identifies as *Mother Clap's Molly House* in Holborn. The Haymarket Theatre, where many popular masquerades were organised, is close to Covent Garden and Spring Gardens—both areas associated with male and female prostitution. In 1781, the actress Elizabeth Inchabald attended a masquerade in male attire and subsequently was said to have "captivated the affections of sundry witless admirers of her own sex."

It was often assumed that any woman who attended a masquerade was doing so to seek sexual liaisons, and female fondness for masquerades became a sign of moral degeneration. Terry Castle (1987) points out that masquerades afforded women a degree of relative freedom in that they were able to approach strangers, strike up conversations, speak coarsely, and generally assume familiarities which were taboo by social standards of correct female decorum. For example, Harriet Wilson (an infamous Regency-period courtesan) who, at the end of her life, wrote her memoirs, and sent each of her former lovers—

including the Duke of Wellington—an unexpurgated version with a note demanding "£200 by return of post, to be left out." Wellington replied with the memorable phrase "publish and be damned." Wilson wrote, "I love a masquerade because a female can never enjoy the same liberty anywhere else."

The masquerade was not without its dangers for women. In one masquerade-themed tale from 1754, the female protagonist is lured from a masquerade by a man who she believes to be her husband. He rapes her, and when her true husband discovers what has transpired, she is exiled from London to his gloomy country seat.

Anti-masquerade tracts often compared the saturnalian spirit of the events to pagan or bacchanalian orgies. Although masquerades frequently had an air of exclusivity about them (both King George II and the Prince of Wales were said to have attended public masquerades), the tickets were priced so that all but the poorest members of society could afford them. Again, the mixing of those of different social positions drew some criticism. One observer, writing in 1718, complained that "the common women of the town" could gain entrance to masquerades and "impertinently" mingle with their betters. The more disreputable elements of society—thieves, gamblers, pimps and prostitutes—were known to frequent masquerades, and prostitutes could present themselves as "women of quality." The inversion of otherwise carefully-segregated social roles occasioned by "dukes dressed as footmen" and "footmen dressed as dukes" meant that the masquerade offered a suspension, albeit temporary, of the rules which governed eighteenth-century life.

21
Bums in Brigantia

The relationships among gender-variance, homoeroticism, magic and mystery traditions have been, until fairly recently, a taboo subject for both occultists and academics alike. Over the last decade or so, interest in both the Northern and Celtic traditions has grown apace, and the latter, in particular, has been romanticised to the point where some people are dismayed if you point out that the Celts kept slaves, ate meat, and indulged in head-hunting. Admittedly, it was my revulsion to this kind of romanticism which first spurred me into investigating some of the aspects of Celtic culture which had been omitted by the revisionists. Another impulse for writing this article is as a counter to what James Martin referred to in *Chaos International* No.16 as "the dispossession of gay and bisexual archetypes." This is not merely (as some might imagine) an exercise in selectively sweeping through history in search of justification for a modern phenomenon, but a desire to demonstrate that gender-variant roles are as much a part of pagan cultural heritage as anything else.

The Germanic Peoples

Call me varg and I'll be arg
call me golden
and I'll be beholden.

— *Wolf-charm*, translated by M.R. Gerstein

The suggestion that gender-variant rites and roles played any part in the Northern Tradition is tantamount to heresy amongst some modern exponents of this current, yet much evidence can be found if one merely lifts the blinkers of Christian influence. It is generally considered that expression of same-sex relationships was frowned upon amongst the Germanic peoples. Surface evidence for this comes via Tacitus, the ambiguity of Loki, and the incident between Sinfjotli and his foe Gundmundr in the Eddas when the former accuses the latter of being a "puff."

The most 'obvious' figure of gender-variant magic and mystery is that of Loki. This complex figure encapsulates both animal transformation and gender variance. In the *Lokasenna* tale, Odinn verbally abuses Loki for allowing himself to be impregnated, calling him *argr*—a crude form of abuse implying that one takes the passive role in intercourse with another man. The noun is *ergi*—and there is the suggestion that anyone repeatedly & willingly doing so is regarded differently from other males. However, the Germanic historian Folke Strom says that *ergi* refers to male practitioner of *seidr*—that it was both the passive role in sodomy & the receptive relationship to the gods was what caused a man to be looked upon, or identify himself as *ergi*. Moreover, in the case of Loki, it is this 'impregnation' which has given birth to Sleipnir, Odinn's eight-legged steed. Loki is interesting in this respect, as the ambiguous relationship between male-oriented and female-oriented magics are most obvious in him. Loki often uses Freyja's feathered cloak to aid his schemes, and it may also be significant that it is only when Loki & Thor submit to feminization that they are able to conquer the giants. Certainly, the motif of the bird-feather cloak is a recurring symbol for both shape-shifting and gender-variance in European traditions.

Odinn, too, has a somewhat ambiguous relationship to the provenance of female-based magics. All of his major acts of power seem to depend on a Goddess. Odinn is said to have worn female clothes on several occasions. One of his titles is *Jalkr* ('Gelding'), and Kveldulf Gundarsson (author of *Teutonic Magic*) suggests that this title relates to Odinn's initiation into the mysteries of *Seidr* Magic—with the implication that Odinn gave himself up to the female principle, becoming a gender-variant shaman. Indeed, in the *Lokasenna* cycle, Loki does respond to Odinn's flyting by drawing attention to Odinn's practice of *seidr*, the ways of which he was instructed by Freyja:

> *"But thou, say they, on Sàm's Isle once wovest spells like a witch: in warlock's shape through the world didst fare: were these womanish ways, I ween."*

There is more to the *Lokasenna* episode than is immediately apparent. Both Loki and Odinn are complex figures, and it should not be forgotten that they are blood-brothers.

From Saxo Grammaticus, a 12th century CE Christian chronicler, comes the information that the god Freyr was served by gender-variant male priests who displayed feminized behaviour and employed bells, which were considered 'unmanly.' They apparently enacted a symbolic sacred marriage in order to "ensure the divine fruitfulness of the season." The Priests of Freyr also performed shape shifting rites with boar masks. The *ergi* priests who practiced *seidr* also performed tasks usually associated with women, such as weaving and childrearing. The quality of their voices was referred to as *seid laeti*, possibly indicating that some of them were castrati. *Seidrmen* were clearly differentiated from men who might occasionally indulge in same-sex relations & take the active role. The key theme here is that in surrendering themselves to passive intercourse, the *ergi* became a channel for the divine.

Some *ergi* men were thought to undergo gender transformation every ninth night, and go out hunting other men in the same manner that a werewolf might hunt victims. The *ergi*-werewolf link appears elsewhere in Germanic, and other European traditions.

Ergi priests would perform inner journeys (often in the form of a falcon) in search of divinatory gnosis, and their chief function was working magic. They were considered able to bestow fame and wealth or take them away, heal and curse, bring lovers together or drive them apart, raise storms, and dull the swords of enemies. Perhaps their reputed power for good or ill goes some way to explaining their rather ambiguous status in Germanic culture, particularly as Christian incursions began to paint sorcery and wonder-working in quite a different light.

According to Tacitus, *ergi* males were drowned in mudholes and marshes; this has been popularly misinterpreted as the fate of anyone who was 'queer' in Germanic culture. Folke Strom however, points out that the male corpses found in peat bogs appear to have been hanged first. A theory suggested by P.V. Glob suggests that the bog corpses are possibly sacrificial deposits, made by worshippers of an early Earth Mother. Glob gives the example of the 'Tollund Man' found with a skillfully plaited noose about his neck, which Glob says indicates to be a replica of a twisted neck ring, a mark of honour of the goddess. There is no complete answer to this problem. Within the worship of Freyja, *ergi* priests appear to have been respected rather than considered criminals. *Ergi* males found in bogs may well have been considered fitting sacrifices to their goddess. However, *ergi* males were being drowned, burned and tortured by the 10th century CE due to the incursion of Christianity. A practitioner of *seidr*,

Eyvinder Kelda was drowned along with other *seidrmen* on the orders of King Olaf Tryggvason, a Christian fanatic, in 998 CE.

During the persecution of *seidrmen* by the Christians, they became labelled as 'heathens.' This is an interesting choice of word, as 'heathen' is etymologically linked to Heidr or Heidi, one of the titles of Freya. Heidr is linked to the Germanic word *heide* ('heath'). According to Diana L. Paxon, the 'heath' is the wilderness outside the Garth, into which the *seidr* practitioners retired to work their magic. Gundarsson describes the *utangards* ('wilderness') as "the realm of disorder...the uncanny and unknown." A wilderness populated by not only outlaws, but also ghosts, trolls and elves.

Margaret C. Ross notes that the Jardarmen rite of blood brotherhood had as its prime symbol the Brisingamen torque of Freyja. It has been suggested that torques were used to strangle male sacrifices to the goddess. The torque came to symbolise *argr* behaviour—the gesture of forming the hands into a ring suggested one had the power to cause another male to submit to intercourse. Ross says that Odin once directed this gesture at Thor, boasting that he could have him whenever he liked. Ross concludes that the Jardarmen rite, as a ceremony of blood brotherhood, may have involved ritualised intercourse between young males and elders to mark entry into an adult male society.

This latter point is interesting in the light of the *ergi*-werewolf link, and the existence of warrior-bands such as the *Vargr*, or wolf-warrior. Some Germanic scholars think it highly probable that initiation into wolf-warrior bands involved initiatory homosexuality. The image of the werewolf has many resonances with initiatory homosexuality— such as the Wolf *(Erastes)*-Lamb *(Eromenes)* initiatory relationship in some areas of Greece; the initiatory trial of 'living like a werewolf' in ancient Sparta; and the unrestrained sexual behaviour of the *luparithe* wolf priests of the Roman Lupercalia. There may be a hidden hint regarding this in the tale of Sinfjotli and Gundmundr. Sinfjotli. is known to have been a member of a wolf-warrior band, whilst Gundmundr is portrayed as a 'female' wolf who has given birth to nine children, of which Sinfjotli is the father. It is possible, even, as Randy Conner (author of *Blossom of Bone)* points out, that Gundmundr was a practitioner of *Seidr.*

The Celts

> *"Although they have good-looking women, they pay very little attention to them, but are really crazy about having sex with men. They are accustomed to sleep on the ground on animal skins and roll around with male bed-mates on both sides. Heedless of their own dignity, they abandon without qualm the bloom of their bodies to others. And the most incredible thing is that they don't think this is shameful. But when they proposition someone, they consider it dishonourable if he doesn't accept the offer!"*

> — Diodorus Siculus (1 BCE)

There is little information extant about gender variance amongst the Celts, but from what we do know, it seems that same sex relations between warriors were not unknown—there is evidence of homosexuality in Celtic warrior bands which were known as *Bleiden* or 'Wolf'. Significantly, despite similar motifs (such as shape-shifting & the wilderness initiation), there was a marked difference between Greek and Celtic homoeroticism in that, unlike the Greeks, the Celts did not consider it shameful that males elected to take the 'passive' role. Diodorus' attitude requires a little explanation, as the ancient Greek attitude to homoeroticism was not as clear-cut as is often thought to be the case. The basic Greek homosexual relationship was between an older man and a youth. The older man admired the younger for his male qualities (beauty, strength, speed, endurance), and the younger man respected the older for his wisdom, experience and command. The older man was expected to train, educate and protect the younger, and in due course the young man grew up and became a friend, rather than a lover-pupil. Both males were expected in due course to marry and father children. These relationships were not deemed to be privately erotic, but were regarded as of great importance to the state, and so supervised by its authorities.

However, some Greek societies strongly disapproved of sexual relationships between men of the same age. Male prostitution was permitted, but practitioners were prohibited from holding office. Sexual relationships between men of the same age (and status) was deemed unnatural because it meant one of the men adopted a passive role, thereby betraying his masculinity. So long as a man retained the 'active' role and his partner was a woman (seen as naturally inferior), a slave (unfree), or a youth (not yet a fully-grown man), then his masculinity was preserved. According to Plutarch, men who did not marry were scorned, ridiculed and punished by Spartan authorities.

Three areas where we can find evidence for gender-variance and homoeroticism include hints on same-sex relationships in the life of Cuchullain, the story of the Men of Ulster, and the myth of Gwydion and Gilvaethy.

Doctor Sandy MacLennan, writing in *Azoth* No.17 (1983) suggests that the Celtic hero Cuchullain's initiation from Cullan the smith, may have had a sexual component. The name Cuchullain means 'Cullan's Hound', and the dog can appear as a symbol of homosexual intercourse. He also notes that in some Irish traditions the Picts came from the region of Scythia, and as Herodotus describes, the Scythians had a cult of shamans called the Enariae, who celebrated the dog days (rising of Sirius) with "sodomitical orgies."

In another instance, Cuchulain & Ferdia were both given warrior training by a legendary female warrior (possibly a goddess) Scathach (Shade). Later, they found themselves on opposite sides of a battle over the brown bull of Cailnge. Ferdia says of Cuchullain:

> "Fast Friend, forest companions,
> we made one bed and slept one sleep in foreign lands after the
>   fray.
> Scathach's pupils, two together, we'd set forth to comb the
>   forest."

Cuchullain slew Ferdia in the battle (there is a possibility that it was accidental), but took his dying friend in his arms and lamented. This has been compared to Achilles' lamentation over Hector, and may represent a paradigmatic example for displaying the ideals of close friendship between warriors.

The tale of the Sickness of the Men of Ulster features the gynandrous horse goddess, Macha, who is associated with shape-shifting. The story is that Macha took for a lover a peasant named Crunnuic, who rashly told the King of the Ulaidh that his 'wife' could run faster than any horse. Macha (disguised) though pregnant, is consequently forced to race against horses. During the race, she suffers great agony and gives birth to children on the track. She reveals her true nature and curses the Men of Ulster so that during moments of crisis, they will become feminized and experience the pangs of childbirth. This curse was effective for nine generations. Jean Markale, author of *Women of the Celts* links this myth to gender transformed shamans, but the aspect of the 'blessing' of such metamorphosis has been lost, she feels, due to the erosion of matrifocal myth.

Another interesting Celtic myth in this respect is the Judgement of Math upon his two nephews:

> *"This was the judgement of Math the King upon his nephews Gwydion and Gilvaethy who stole the pigs of Pryderi. He transformed one into a doe and the other into a stag, and sent them forth into the wilderness. They returned a year later, and brought before Math a faun. Math again transformed the nephews, the doe became a boar, and the stag became a sow, and the faun he transformed into a handsome boy, Hydwn. A year later, they returned with a young pig. This time, Math transformed the boar into a she-wolf and the sow into a wolf, and the young pig into a boy with auburn hair; Hychdwn the Tall. The final time they returned with a wolf cub, whom Math transformed into Bleiddwn the Wolfling, and then he relented, and restored the nephews to their true shapes."[1]*

There is an echo here, of the Greek wilderness initiation rite mentioned above, certainly of the relationship among animals, shape-shifting, initiations and homosexual behaviour. Christian-based commentaries on this episode maintain that as the nephews had broken the law, they were sent out to live "like animals," but I feel there is an element of an earlier myth here. It would be interesting to look further into the Celtic Mythic associations of the three animals, the Stag, the Boar, and the Wolf. The role shifts between the nephews from male to female animals, and the birth of the "handsome boys" which Math raised as his own, are also intriguing. This myth contains elements of shape-shifting, shamanism and the wilderness initiation.

---

[1] Paraphrased from *The Island of the Mighty* by Evangeline Walton.

While the experience is, on the surface, a 'punishment,' Gilvaethy is endowed with great strength as a result of the ordeal, whilst Gwydion is thereafter renowned for his cunning. Math certainly plays the role of an initiator-mentor in this myth, and it is played throughout this entire cycle that Math's power stems from the land itself—from Nature, rather than mere human authority.

There is also the figure of the Irish *filidh* to consider: a poet, story-teller, singer, historian and practitioner of divination. This bardic figure appears to have had many shamanic aspects, and is linked to rituals involving eating the raw flesh of a sacrificed bull, drinking its blood, and sleeping in its hide—to inspire prophetic dreams. The *filidh* were considered to be representatives of the Goddess, and there is some evidence that in this respect, there was a 'romantic attach-ment' between a King and the *filidh*, in which the *filidh* played the receptive role, although it is not clear as to whether there was an erotic dimension to this relationship. A cloak of bird-feathers is thought to be one of their symbols of office.

Transgression & Transformation

Nine, the number of the Moon, and of female mysteries in gen-eral, also appears time and time again in association with these trans-formations. There is a Greek legend concerning a secret ritual held yearly atop Mount Lykaion, at the conclusion of which a man was transformed into a wolf for nine years. This legend is an extension of the original wilderness transgression of Lykaon, who was trans-formed by Zeus into a wolf. Nine is also a prominent number in the Celtic and Germanic mysteries—Odinn hung from the World-Tree for Nine days, for example.

A recurrent theme which has emerged from this discussion is the link between gender-variance, lycanthropy and 'outlaw' status. This theme is concerned with the power of the blurred, or liminal, image. All belong to the realm of disorder which lies beyond ordered society. This is the case for the Greek lycanthropes, the Celtic *Bleiden,* the Germanic *vargr* (from which depend the words 'vagabond' and 'vagrant'), and the Anglo-Saxon term for outlaw: wolf's-head. The wolf-image relates to the paradoxical theme of sacred transgressors— those who are outlaws, yet also figures of myth, fear and respect. Both the skin-changer and the gender-variant male are 'sacred outlaw' figures which show a wide cross-cultural dispersal.

Queerying Histories: Bibliography

Bleys, Rudi. 1996. *The Geography of Perversion: Male-to-Male Sexual Behaviour Outside the West and the Ethnographic Imagination 1750–1918.* Cassell.

Braude, Ann. 2001. *Radical Spirits: Spiritualism and Women's Rights in Nineteenth-Century America.* Indiana University Press.

Carpenter, Edward. 1919. *Intermediate Types Among Primitive Folk.* George Allen and Unwin Ltd.

Castle, Terry. 1986. *Masquerade and Civilisation: The Carnivalesque in Eighteenth-Century English Culture and Fiction.* Stanford University Press.

Castle, Terry. 1995. *The Female Thermometer: Eighteenth-Century Culture and the Invention of the Uncanny.* Oxford University Press.

Castelli, Elizabeth & Rodman, Rosamund (eds.) 2001. *Women, gender, religion: a reader.* Palgrave.

Clarke, Bruce. 2001. *Energy Forms: Allegory and Science in the Era of Classical Thermodynamics.* University of Michigan Press.

Clouston, T.S., M.D. 'Female Education from a Medical Point of View' in *The Popular Science Monthly,* December 1883, Vol. 24, No.10. Bonnier Corporation.

Connor, Randy. 1993. *Blossom of Bone.* HarperSanFransisco.

Darwin, Charles. 1871. *The Descent of Man and Selection in Relation to Sex.* Volume II. John Murray.

Dixon, Joy. 2001. *Divine Feminine: Theosophy and Feminism in England.* John Hopkins University Press.

Duberman, Martin B. (ed.) 1997. *A Queer World: The Center for Lesbian and Gay Studies Reader.* New York University Press.

Ellingson, Ter J. 2001. *The Myth of the Noble Savage.* University of California Press.

Evans, Arthur. 1978. *Witchcraft and the Gay Counterculture.* Fag Rag Books.

Findlen, Paula; Roworth, Wendy Wassyng; Sama, Catherine M. 2009. *Italy's Eighteenth Century: Gender and Culture in the Age of the Grand Tour.* Stanford University Press.

Flaherty, Gloria. 1992. *Shamanism and the Eighteenth Century.* Princeton University Press.

Fryer, Jonathan. 1978. *Isherwood: A Biography.* Doubleday & Co., Inc.

Galvan, Jill. 2010. *The Sympathetic Medium: Feminine Channeling, the Occult and Communication Technologies 1859–1919.* Cornell University Press.

Gay, Susan. 'The Future of Women' in *Lucifer,* October 1890. Vol. VII, No.38.

Gilman, Sander L.; King, Helen; Porter, Roy; Rousseau, G.S.; Showalter, Helen. 1993. *Hysteria Beyond Freud.* University of California Press.

Gold, Barri J. 2010. *ThermoPoetics: Energy in Victorian Literature and Science.* The MIT Press.

Gutiérrez, Ramón A. Warfare, 'Homosexuality, and Gender Status Among American Indian Men in the Southwest' in Foster,

Thomas (ed.) *Long Before Stonewall: Histories of Same-Sex Sexuality in Early America.* New York University Press, 2007.

Gyrus. 2009. *War & the Noble Savage: A Critical Inquiry into Recent Accounts of Violence Amongst Uncivilised Peoples.* Dreamflesh Press.

Harvey, Karen. 2004. *Reading Sex in the Eighteenth Century: Bodies and Gender in English Erotic Culture.* Cambridge University Press.

Hitchcock, Tim. 1997. *English Sexualities, 1700–1800.* Palgrave Macmillan.

Horswell, Michael J. 2005. *Decolonizing the sodomite: queer tropes of sexuality in colonial Andean culture.* University of Texas Press.

Howson, Gerald. 2006. *Thief-Taker General: Jonathan Wild and the Emergence of Crime and Corruption as a Way of Life in Eighteenth-Century England.* Transaction Publishers.

Johnson, Mark. 2009. "Transgression and the Making of 'Western' Sexual Sciences" in Donnan, Magowan (eds.) *Transgressive sex: subversion and control in erotic encounters.* Berghahn Books.

Jordan, Sarah. 2004. *The Anxieties of Idleness: Idleness in Eighteenth Century British Literature and Culture.* Bucknell University Press.

Laqueur, Thomas. 1990. *Making sex: body and gender from the Greeks to Freud.* Harvard University Press.

Maccubbin, Robert P. (ed.) 1987. *'Tis nature's fault: unauthorized sexuality during the Enlightenment.* Cambridge University Press.

Mudge, Bradford. (ed.). 2004. *When Flesh Becomes Word: An Anthology of Early Eighteenth-Century Libertine Literature.* Oxford University Press.

Murphy, Patricia. 2006. *In Science's Shadow: Literary Constructions of Late Victorian Women.* University of Missouri Press.

Owen, Alex. 2004. *The Darkened Room: Women, Power, and Spiritualism in Late Victorian England.* Chicago University Press.

Owen, Alex. 2004. *Place of Enchantment: British Occultism and the Culture of the Modern.* University of Chicago Press.

Owen, Alex. 2004. *The Darkened Room: Women, Power and Spiritualism in Late Victorian England.* University of Chicago Press.

Phillips, Kim M. & Reay, Barry. 2011. *Sex Before Sexuality: A Premodern History.* Polity Press.

Price, Neil S. (ed.). 2001. *The Archaeology of Shamanism.* Routledge.

Rabinach, Anson. 1990. *The Human Motor: Energy, Fatigue, and the Origins of Modernity.* Basic Books, Inc.

Reynolds, J. Russell. 1868. (ed.) *A System of Medicine.* Macmillan and Co.

Rocke, Michael. 1996. *Forbidden Friendships: Homosexuality and Male Culture in Renaissance Florence.* Oxford University Press.

Roscoe, Will. 2000. *Changing Ones: Third and Fourth Genders in Native North America.* St. Martin's Press.

Rousseau, G.S. 1991. *Perilous enlightenment: pre- and post-modern discourses: sexual, historical.* Manchester University Press.

Rousseau, G.S. Porter, R. (eds.) 1987. *Sexual Underworlds of the Enlightenment.* Manchester University Press.

Russett, Cynthia Eagle. 1991. *Sexual Science: The Victorian Construction of Womanhood.* Harvard University Press.

Sergent, Bernard. 1987. *Homosexuality in Greek Myth.* Athlone.

Simon, Linda. 2004. *Dark Light: Electricity and Anxiety from the Telegraph to the X-ray.* Houghton Mifflin Harcourt.

Swiney, Frances. 1907. *The Bar of Isis: The Law of the Mother.* Open Road Publishing.

Trumbach, Randolph. 1998. *Sex and the Gender Revolution: Heterosexuality and the third gender in Enlightenment London v.1.* University of Chicago Press.

Vangaard, Thorkil. 1969. *Phallos: A Symbol and its History in the Male World.* Jonathan Cape.

Wallace, Lee. 2003. *Sexual Encounters: Pacific Texts, Modern Sexualities.* Cornell University.

Walton, Evangeline. 1970. *The Island of the Mighty.* Ballantine Books.

Wheeler, Roxanne. 2000. *The Complexion of Race: Categories of Difference in Eighteenth-Century British Culture.* University of Pennsylvania Press.

Wilson, Kathleen. (ed.) 2004. *A New Imperial History: Culture, Identity and Modernity in Britain and the Empire, 1660–1840.* State University of New York.

About the Author

Phil Hine has been a practising Occultist for over forty-five years, with a career spanning Wicca, Ritual Magic, Chaos Magic and nondual Tantra. Together with Rodney Orpheus, he co-created and edited the UK's first monthly Pagan magazine, *Pagan News* (1988–1992). He is a former initiate of the Illuminates of Thanateros, The Esoteric Order of Dagon, and the Arcane & Mystical Order of the Knights of Shamballa (AMOOKOS). In the 1980s he was an activist in Pagan networks such as *PaganLink* and *HOBLink*—the UK's first network for LGBTQ occult practitioners. He lives in London, England.

His books include *Condensed Chaos: An Introduction to Chaos Magic*; *Prime Chaos: Adventures in Chaos Magic*; *The Pseudonomicon*; and *Hine's Varieties: Chaos & Beyond* (all published by The Original Falcon Press). He has also self-published lectures on the history of Chakras and Possession in early Tantric literature. In 2019 he founded Twisted Trunk, a small press specializing in publishing translations of rare Tantric texts.

His most recent work can be found at enfolding.org.

OTHER TITLES BY PHIL HINE

CONDENSED CHAOS
Introduction to Chaos Magic
Foreword by Peter J. Carroll

"The most concise statement of the logic of modern magic. Magic, in the light of modern physics, quantum theory, and probability theory is now approaching science. We hope that a result of this will be a synthesis so that science will become more magical, and magic more scientific."
— William S. Burroughs, author of *Naked Lunch*

"A tour de force."
— Ian Read, Editor, *Chaos International*

PRIME CHAOS
Adventures in Chaos Magic

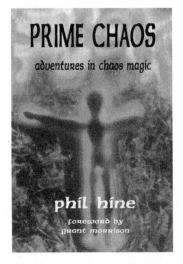

An overview of the fastest-growing school of modern occultism, Chaos Magic. Simple and effective techniques for becoming proficient in practical magic, including ritual magic, sorcery, invocation, possession and evocation. *Prime Chaos* also explores some of the lighter— and darker—aspects of modern occultism, and presents new ideas for developing magical techniques.

"I wish I'd written this book!"
— Peter J. Carroll, author of *Liber Kaos* and *Psybermagick*

OTHER TITLES BY PHIL HINE

HINE'S VARIETIES
Chaos & Beyond

Divided thematically into sections—Chaos Magic, Tantra, Sexualities, Practice, Paganisms, Histories, and Fiction—each is prefaced by autobiographical writings in which Phil reflects on the early beginnings of his magical path, and how his perspectives have changed over time. Ranging from explorations of esoteric practice, magical sexuality, and independent scholarship, *Hine's Varieties* offers a unique window into the life and spiritual journey of a master magician.

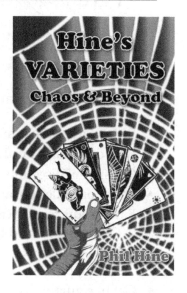

THE PSEUDONOMICON

Each god brings its own madness. To know the god—to be accepted by it, to feel its mysteries—you have to let that madness wash over and through you. This isn't in books of magic. Why? For one thing, it's all too easily forgotten; for another, you must find it out for yourself. So why Cthulhu—High Priest of the Great Old Ones—lying dreaming "death's dream" in the sunken city, forgotten through layers of time and water? It sounds so simple to say that I merely heard his "call"—but I did. Gods do not, generally, have a lot to say, but what they do say, is worth listening to.

THE *Original* FALCON PRESS

Invites You to Visit Our Website:
originalfalcon.com

At our website you can:

- Browse the online catalog of all of our great titles
- Find out what's available and what's out of stock
- Get special discounts
- Order our titles through our secure online server
- Find products not available anywhere else including:
  - One of a kind and limited availability products
  - Special packages
  - Special pricing
- Get free gifts
- Join our email list for advance notice of New Releases and Special Offers
- Find out about book signings and author events
- Send email to our authors
- Read excerpts of many of our titles
- Find links to our authors' websites
- Discover links to other weird and wonderful sites
- And much, much more

Visit us today at originalfalcon.com

Made in the USA
Middletown, DE
30 September 2024

61689871R00116